CASS LIBRARY OF WEST INDIAN STUDIES
No. 23

AN HISTORICAL ACCOUNT
OF THE
ISLAND OF SAINT VINCENT

A list of titles in the
CASS LIBRARY OF WEST INDIAN STUDIES
appears at the end of this volume

AN

HISTORICAL ACCOUNT

OF THE

ISLAND OF SAINT VINCENT

BY

CHARLES SHEPHARD

Routledge
Taylor & Francis Group

LONDON AND NEW YORK

First Published 1971 by
Frank Cass & Co. Ltd

2 Park Square, Milton Park, Abingdon, Oxon OX14 4RN
711 Third Avenue, New York, NY 10017, USA

Routledge is an imprint of the Taylor & Francis Group, an informa business

First issued in paperback 2016

British Library Cataloguing in Publication Data:

A catalogue record for this book is available
from the British Library

Library of Congress Cataloging-in-Publication Data:

A catalog record for this book is available
from the Library of Congress

ISBN 13: 978-0-7146-1951-4 (hbk)
ISBN 13: 978-1-138-97605-4 (pbk)

AN

HISTORICAL ACCOUNT

OF THE

ISLAND OF SAINT VINCENT.

BY

CHARLES SHEPHARD, ESQ.

LONDON:

PRINTED BY W. NICOL, CLEVELAND ROW, ST. JAMES'S.

SOLD BY RIDGWAY AND SONS, PICCADILLY; ROBINSON
AND SON, LIVERPOOL; AND SMITH AND SON, GLASGOW.

1831.

TO

THE SURVIVORS

OF

THE CARIB WAR,

THIS RECORD OF THEIR SERVICES,

AND OF

THEIR DEPARTED COMPANIONS IN ARMS,

IS RESPECTFULLY INSCRIBED.

LIST OF SUBSCRIBERS.

Agassiz, Rev. R. Saint Vincent.
Allan, George,   ditto.

Barbados, Right Rev. Lord Bishop of.   2 copies.
Baynham, E. Bermuda.
Bell, Simpson, Bristol.
Berenger, Viscountess Monod de, Rue Faubourg, St.
          Honoré, Paris.
Billinghurst, Joseph, Saint Vincent.   3 copies.
Bolton, John, Duke Street, Liverpool.
Bowra, Thomas, Saint Vincent.   2 copies.
Bridgewater, Symonds, Dominica.
Bubb, Henry, Saint Vincent.
Bushe, Robert, Trinidad.
Beresford, John, Saint Vincent.   2 copies.
Brown, James W.   ditto.   2 copies.

Cardigan, Earl of, Portman Square.
Cadiz, J. J. Trinidad.
Clarke, John, Saint Vincent.

Cayley, Thomas, Saint Vincent.
Cockerton, John, Trinidad.

Colonial Department of His Majesty's Secretary of States' Office. 4 copies.
Colquhoun, James, St. James's Place.
Coningham, Walter, Saint Vincent.
Conyers, Charles, Demerary. 2 copies.
Crawford, John D. Saint Vincent.
Cropper, Edward,   ditto.
Cropper, George,   ditto.   2 copies.
Cropper, John, Liverpool.
Cropper, N. Bassnett, Saint Vincent.
Cropper, Thomas,   ditto.
Cropper, William,   ditto.
Cruikshank, Alexander, Stracathro, N. B.
Cumming, Alexander, Saint Vincent.

Darrell, George R. Saint Vincent. 2 copies.
Dawson, William,   ditto.
Dickinson, John,   ditto.
Dickinson, William T. ditto.
Dixon, Charles, Captain Royal Engineers.
Douglas, Charlotte, Saint Vincent. 2 copies.
Drape, John,   ditto.   10 copies.
Denton, William, London.

Eckstein, John, Trinidad.

Featherstone, Joseph, Saint Vincent.
Forbes, J. H. Ely Place, London.
Fraser, Thomas, Saint Vincent.
French, James Charles, Saint Vincent.
Fuller, Henry, Trinidad.

Glanville, Henry J. Dominica.
Gloster, Henry, Trinidad.
Gordon, John, 5 Argyll Street, Liverpool.
Gordon, John, Liverpool.
Grant, James, Saint Vincent.
Guilding, Rev. Lansdown, ditto.

Hackshaw, H. Gloucester Place, Portman Square.
Haffey, Henry, Bath. 3 copies.
Hanley, W. Trinidad.
Harrison, John, Saint Vincent.
Hartley, George, ditto. 2 copies.
Hobson, Pemberton, ditto. 2 copies.
Hollocombe, E. J. ditto.
Hoyes, Lewis, Grenada.
Huskisson, George, Saint Vincent.
Hodder, J. F. M. Hodder's Field.
Horne, John, Saint Vincent.
Hyde, Mr. Dorset Street, Dorset Square.

Jones, James, Saint Vincent.
Johnstone, Lewis, J. C. Trinidad.

Kirkwall, Right Hon. Viscountess, Weymouth Street.

Lewis, John, Saint Vincent.
Littledale, Johnson, ditto. 2 copies.
Llanos, Francisco, Trinidad.
Lockhart, James P. Dominica.

Mac Arthur, John, Saint Vincent.
M'Kenzie, William, ditto.

M'Leod, Alexander,   ditto.

M'Nair, Charles,   ditto.

Mackworth, Herbert, Trinidad.

Mason, Colonel, Jordan Street, Edge Hill, Liverpool.

Maxwell, John, Saint Vincent.

Melville, Alexander, Staff Surgeon, ditto.

Melville, John, ditto.

Melville, Thomas, ditto.   2 copies.

Miller, John, Trinidad.

Mitchell, George H. Saint Vincent,

Morrin, Samuel,   ditto. 2 copies.

Mowbray, John,   ditto.

Munro, Gilbert, Saint Vincent.

Murray, Right Hon. Sir George, G. C. B. ditto.

Neverson, Samuel, Liverpool.

Newbold, Nathan, Saint Vincent.   2 copies.

Owen, Hugh, Liverpool.

Parry, Venerable Archdeacon, Antigua.

Ponsonby, William Glenn, Saint Vincent.   2 copies.

Ponsonby, John,   ditto.

Prest, John,   ditto.

Prest, Edward, Heslington, near York.

Prest, William, York.

Primrose, Rev. Dr. Preston Pans, N. B.

Primrose, John, Saint Vincent.

Prosser, David, Bristol.

Punnett, Christopher, Saint Vincent.

Questel, Drewry, Saint Vincent.
Questel, Harriet,   ditto.

Ramus, William George, Tobago.
Rees, Richard, Saint Vincent.   2 copies.
Rickard, David,   ditto.
Robertson, Richard, St. Vincent.
Robeson, George, Fort Adjutant, ditto.
Ross, Henry James, Lincoln's Inn.
Ross, John Pemberton, Saint Vincent.
Rumbold, C. E., M. P. Harley Street.   10 copies.
Russell, Robert, Saint Vincent.

Stewart, C. D. Saint Vincent.
Sanderson, E. D. Trinidad.
Sanderson, John, ditto.
Scott, William Rose, Saint Vincent.   2 copies.
Seymour, John Vobe,   ditto.
Sharpe, Edward, York Place.
Sheill, William, Montserratt.   12 copies.
Skelly, Adam, Saint Vincent.
Small, John, Junior, ditto.
Sprott, William,   ditto.
St. Hill, Thomas, Trinidad.
Stafford, John, Saint Vincent.
Stowe, William,   ditto.   2 copies.
Stedman, John, Chester.
Struth, Sir William, President of Saint Vincent. 2 copies.
Sutherland, Duncan F. Saint Vincent.
Sutherland, Ewen B.

Sutherland, George M.
Sutherland, James, Saint Vincent.
Sutherland, Robert,   ditto.
Swift, Fred. J. Trinidad.
Stewart, John, Saint Vincent.   2 copies.
Symon, James, ditto.

Taylor, Sackville M. Saint Vincent.

Vanheyningen, G. Saint Vincent.

Wall, Daniel, Saint Vincent.
Warner, Ashton, Chief Judge, Trinidad.
Warner, Mrs. Ashton,   ditto.
Warner, Charles W.   ditto.
Wickham, Lieut. Richard S. Barbados.
Williamson, James, Gray's Inn Square.   2 copies.
Williamsons, Miss, Bedale, Yorkshire.
Weller, Francis, R. A. Ceylon.

ADVERTISEMENT.

The Work now offered to the Public was undertaken at the request of several Gentlemen of the Colony, who were anxious that the particular circumstances attendant on the Insurrection in 1795, should be preserved in a convenient form, and with more minuteness, than has hitherto been done in the Historical Narratives of the West Indian Islands.

It may probably be considered, that too great an importance has been attached to the preservation, and subsequent culture of a small Island of the Antilles, but the proprietors of Saint Vincent are actuated by a different feeling; they are conscious of the exertions, the sacrifices, the devotedness of the Inhabitants in 1795, although these were on a small scale, yet they were made for their existence and their property, and to them, the Narrative is as deeply interesting, as the Annals of European warfare are to the general reader; hence the occasional

minuteness of detail, the constant insertion of
names, where the perspicuity of the Narrative
does not require it, will be pardoned from this
explanation of the particular object of the
Work.

The Book must necessarily be a compilation.
Bryan Edwards' Work, and the Narrative inserted in Dr. Coke's History of the West Indies,
have been principally followed, but with considerable alterations, for the Author has been
fortunate enough to obtain several Manuscript
Diaries of events made at the time, and has
thus been enabled to correct many errors; he
has also ascertained many interesting particulars from resident survivors, to whom he is
highly indebted for the liberal and unreserved
communications they have always afforded.
During the progress of the Work, however, the
mortality among the elder inhabitants, and
especially in the year 1829, was very great,
and many of his well wishers have sunk into
the grave. It may be recorded as a singular
and unprecedented circumstance in Colonial
annals, that the Governor, (Sir Charles Brisbane) the President of the Council, (Hon.
Robert Gordon) the Speaker, (Hon. John

Dalzell) and the Chief Justice, (Hon. John Henry Hobson) should all have died within the short space of three months, without the prevalence of any epidemic disease.

To render the Work generally useful, a number of Tables and Returns have been collected from authentic sources, and a short summary of West Indian Chronology has been compiled. The Index to Byres's Map, has also been reprinted with some additions, as the Map has been latterly republished, and is in general use; an accurate Map however is still a desideratum, which the present Crown and Colony Surveyors are eminently qualified to supply.

The mode of Colonial cultivation has been of late years so fully entered into by different Authors, that any further observations must become mere repetition; therefore only a few interesting statistical details relative to the expences of estates, and the prices of produce, have been inserted. The same may be said of the long agitated question of Slavery, which has been exhausted by Mr. Barclay, Mr. Barham, Mr. M'Queen, Mr. Macdonnell and others. The Manners and Customs of Tropical Life have been depicted by Dr. Pinckard, Mr. Coleridge, a Resident's Sketches, and the Author of Marly, with the happiest effect, and require no further illustration.

The Author returns his most grateful thanks to his numerous Subscribers for their patronage and support. If any Names should be omitted in the List, he trusts it will be attributed to the difficulty of procuring them from the adjacent Islands in time to be forwarded to the Printer in London, and also that his absence from Europe will be an excuse for any errors in composition, which, though conspicuous in print, will escape the most attentive observer in manuscript.

Saint Vincent,
August, 1830.

CONTENTS.

b

CONTENTS.

SECTION V.

SECTION VI.

SECTION VII.

SECTION VIII.

CONTENTS.

SECTION IX.

Form of the present Government—Courts of Justice—
Slave Laws—Registry Acts—Commerce—Ecclesiastical
Establishment—Education—Colonial Deficiencies, p. 194

SECTION X.

APPENDIX.

APPENDIX

HISTORICAL ACCOUNT, &c.

SECTION I.

*Topographical description—Soil—Climate—Roads—
Kingstown—Botanic Garden—Parishes—Population—Revenue—Coin—Garrison—Militia.*

SAINT VINCENT was discovered by Columbus
on the 22d day of January, A. D. 1498, and was
named from that circumstance, it being St.
Vincent's day in the Spanish Calendar.* It is a
very beautiful, healthy, and fertile island, lying

* Saint Vincent was deacon of Saragossa. Gibbon however thinks he was attached to a church, either at Evora or
Beia, from the circumstance of the adjoining cape being
named after him, he lived about the end of the third age,
under the Emperors Diocletian and Maximian; he was
tortured and put to death by Datianus, the Governor of
Spain, January 22d, A. D. 305, who endeavoured to root
out Christianity in that country. An account of his suf-
ferings is to be found in Tillemont Memoires Ecclesias-
tiques, Vol. V. Part II. 58. See Gibbon, Chap. XVI.

B

SECT. 1. in 13° 10′ 15″ N. latitude, and 60° 30′ 57″ W. longitude, it is about eighteen and one half miles long, and eleven and one quarter wide, and contains eighty-four thousand two hundred and eighty-six* acres of land, of which, at present, about thirty-five thousand acres are in cultivation; its principal features are lofty mountains in the central parts of the island, clothed with immense trees, diverging in ridges towards the sea of a less elevated description, and intersected by deep ravines in the interior, which gradually widen on the approach to the shore, and become vallies capable of cultivation, in general well supplied with water; this feature is principally descriptive of the north-western side of the island. On the north-east the surface is more level and less broken, and there is a large tract of land at the base of the Souffriere mountain, which forms an extensive plain of upwards of six thousand acres, gradually declining towards the sea, and is the most productive land in the colony. The Soil in the vallies is a rich tenacious loam, and occasionally a fine black mould; on the higher regions it assumes a more sandy

Soil.

* For a more particular detail, see the Appendix No. I.

character, and is less fertile; the lands ad- joining the Souffriere are also clay at the bottom, but the surface having been covered with the sand ejected by the volcano in 1812, it presents the feature of a loose porous superficies. The character of this island is decidedly volcanic, traces of strata which have undergone the action of fire, are visible every where, and huge masses of rock, displaced from their original situations, indicate the powerful agency which alone could have effected such a change, and it is said by those skilled in geological researches, that there is not a primitive rock in the island, an opinion which is supported by branches of trees and other substances, being frequently discovered in large masses of rock at considerable depths, which must at one time have been in a state of fusion; a remarkable instance is to be seen at the tunnel at Grand Sable.

The average Temperature through the year, may be stated at $81\frac{1}{2}$, the air is remarkably elastic and salubrious, the seasons are, in common with all tropical situations, divided into wet and dry, the former commencing with the full moon in May, which is generally preceded

SECT. 1. by thunder, but the variations in the fall of rain are very considerable ; the latter season begins about November, but the elevation of the mountains is so great, that the island is very generally refreshed by cooling showers, and hence is the consequent fertility of the soil.*
The prevailing winds are from the north-east, but at the equinox gales from the southward, and westward, are occasionally experienced. The length of the day varies from 12ʰ 46′ to 11ʰ 54′, and the variation of the needle may be estimated at 2° 50′, East.

Roads.   The Highways on the windward coast are tolerably good for twenty-six miles, their trace in general is near to the sea side, except in cases of high land, when it is necessary to pass along the indentations of the vallies. On the leeward coast, for a distance of twenty-three miles, they are much inferior, the hills being much higher, the circuity of the trace is proportionally increased ; the latter are little frequented, the passage by sea in canoes, being more easy and commodious. The highways are kept in repair by the proprietors of the estates who have adjoining portions allotted them by an Act of the

* See Appendix, Nos. II. and III.

C.D. Stewart Delin.

S.H. Alcock Sculp.

FORT CHARLOTTE SAINT VINCENT.

Published by Kittenny & Son Piccadilly.

Legislature, on which they are required to ex-
pend an estimated quantity of labour, and for
which they are allowed a certain sum from the
treasury, on a certificate from the Way-wardens
of the parish, who are nominated by the Justices at the February Sessions in each year.

The Island is divided into five parishes, Saint
George, Charlotte, Saint Andrew, Saint David,
and Saint Patrick. Within the first, stands the
Capital, KINGSTOWN ;* it is situated near the
south-western extremity of the Island, at the
bottom of a deep bay, about one mile wide,
and is protected by a battery on the south, or
Cane Garden Point, and by Fort Charlotte on
the north-west, which is the chief defence of
the Island; it is situated on a rock, about six
hundred feet above the level of the sea, and is
well fortified. It contains barracks for six hundred men, and has thirty-four pieces of artillery
of different descriptions, besides several out-
works, for the protection of detached buildings.

The town consists of three streets, nearly a
mile long parallel to the sea, intersected by six

* For the accurate and spirited views of the fort and
the town of Kingstown, the author is indebted to his friend
Charles D. Stewart, Esq. Acting Marshal of the colony.

SECT. 1. others. There are about three hundred houses,
the lower stories are in general built with stone
or brick, and the upper of wood, with shingled
roofs ; but there are a number of small wooden
houses, which, however convenient they may
be for the lower classes, give an air of poverty
and inferiority to the whole. Three streams
flow across the town, and add considerably to
its cleanliness. The public buildings are substantial, but not elegant. The Church is a large
heavy brick building, capable of containing two
thousand persons, it has an excellently toned
organ, a splendid chandelier, very handsome
pulpit, and bishop's throne. The expences of
this building, which was opened for divine service in 1820, amounted to upwards of forty-
seven thousand pounds, currency, of which
Government contributed five thousand pounds
sterling, out of the purchase money of the
Carib lands ; the old building was destroyed by
the hurricane in 1780.

The Court House is built of stone, and contains two rooms on the upper story appropriated for the sittings of the Council and
Assembly, with two Committee Rooms ; below
the Courts of Justice are held. Here also are

the Public Offices of the Registrar, and Mar- shal; this building stands in front of the Market Place, and is inclosed with an iron railing; behind it the Gaol, the Cage and the Treadmill are placed. In the front close to the sea side, stand the Market House, and the depot for the Militia Arms. The Wesleyan Missionaries have a commodious wooden Chapel, and the Romanists have commenced a brick Church.

About one mile from Kingstown, is the Bo- Botanic tanic Garden, this establishment was first com- Garden. menced in 1763, and consists of about thirty acres of land, of which, sixteen were formerly cultivated with great care. Dr. Young, Dr. Anderson, Mr. Lockhead, and Mr. Caley were successively Superintendants, at a liberal salary from the Government, and with a supply of twelve Negroes; the control of it was entrusted to the Secretary at War, to whom regular reports were transmitted. Here almost every species of the vegetable world, which the hand of nature has bestowed on the West India Islands for use and beauty, for food and luxury abounded, and many valuable exotics were imported from the East Indies, and South America.

SECT. 1.   The Mango, and the Cinnamon, which were introduced by Lord Rodney in Jamaica in 1782, were also sent to this establishment, also some of the original bread fruit plants, brought by Captain Bligh from Otaheite in 1793, and through the zeal and activity of Dr. Anderson, two Nutmeg Trees were procured from Cayenne in 1809. The Clove was obtained from Martinico as early as 1787, where it was brought from the East Indies; great care was displayed in the cultivation of these spices, which are now so generally circulated through the Island, that in a few years they must become abundant.* But on the death of Mr. Lockhead in 1814, the prosperity of this establishment began to decline; his successor was discontented with his appointment, and disagreed with the inhabitants, and harrassed his superiors at the War Office by reiterated complaints. Hence the Government embraced the opportunity of

---

* The Rev. Lansdown Guilding has published a short account of this garden, with a catalogue of all the plants, to which the Botanical reader is referred : it is to be hoped that this work is a prelude only to a more general description of West Indian plants, which this gentleman is so eminently qualified to give.

directing a great proportion of the plants to sect. 1. be removed to Trinidad, and discontinued the allowances.

The land was offered to the Colony on the condition of erecting a Government House; for some few years eight hundred pounds currency, was annually expended by the Legislature in partially maintaining the Garden, and preserving the remaining trees, but in 1828, this allowance was discontinued, and the sum of four thousand five hundred pounds was voted to the Governor, for the purpose of erecting a cottage there, which was completed, and about three acres conveyed to Trustees for the use of the Governor for the time being. This is at present, the only residence for the Chief Magistrate, the old Government House in Kingstown having long been in a dilapidated state.

SAINT GEORGE's Parish extends from Kings- Parishes. town, north river to the Jambou, and contains nine thousand three hundred and thirty-seven acres of land in sugar estates; it has seven rivers capable of turning mills; the different ridges in this parish having been cleared of their wood, by the earlier settlers, the clouds

SECT. 1. are attracted by the more lofty mountains in the interior; and it has been deemed prudent to preserve the timber on an elevated situation, called the King's Hill,* from future destruction, by an especial Act of the Legislature.

At three miles from Kingstown is the small town of Calliaqua, consisting of fifty-nine houses, and four hundred inhabitants, its chief attraction is the commodious harbour, and very convenient beach for shipping produce. There is a singularly insulated rock on the north western side, two hundred and sixty feet above the level of the sea, on the top of which, Fort Duvernette is constructed; it is ascended by a staircase cut out of the solid stone. On Dor-

---

* Baron Humboldt's remarks on this subject ought to be deeply impressed on the mind of every proprietor. " By felling the trees that cover the tops and the sides of the mountains, men in every climate prepare at once two calamities for future generations, the want of fuel, and the scarcity of water; where forests are destroyed as they are every where in America by the European planters with an imprudent precipitation, the springs are entirely dried up or become less abundant, the beds of the rivers remaining dry during a part of the year, are converted into torrents whenever great rains fall on the heights." Pers. Narrative, Vol. IV. p. 142.

setshire Hill there are barracks for troops, but in such a dilapidated state, as not to be habitable.   Some distance above Calliaqua, towards the interior is the Vigie, (or look out) a commanding situation, rendered memorable from the events of the Insurrection.   The different ridges are here concentrated into one elevation with three conical hills, where the Caribs fixed their camp.   Eastward is the very extensive valley of Maniaqua, which has only one singular cleft, or opening, with almost perpendicular sides, through which the river Jambou flows to the sea.*   Some persons have conjectured that this valley is an exhausted crater, which has been thus drained of its waters; but the position is too low to maintain this hypothesis, as the volcanic craters in all the Islands, are situated on the most lofty mountains.

CHARLOTTE Parish is bounded on the south by St. George's, and northerly by uncultivable

* Here is a majestic cabbage tree, (Areca oleracea) which in 1814 was ascertained to be one hundred and fifty-six feet high by trigonometrical measurement, this is considerably higher than Mr. Coleridge has admitted,—though the existence of Ligon's three hundred feet trees is by no means contended for.

lands, it contains eleven thousand eight hundred and forty-nine acres in cultivation, and that part of it called the Carib country, which was only partially settled in 1804, is the most productive in the Island. The southern part consists of a portion of General Monckton's grant of four thousand acres, which he sold for thirty thousand pounds sterling, and which was subsequently sold in lots by the speculators. This parish is so well supplied with rivers, notwithstanding several were absorbed at the time of the eruption of the Souffriere, that all the mills are worked by water; and the estates are generally larger than in the other parishes. A tunnel of two hundred feet long was cut through Mount Young in 1813, which greatly improved the means of communication with the newly settled country; and a stupendous work was afterwards undertaken by the owner of Grand Sable Estate, in cutting another tunnel through the same mountain, lower down, and nearer the sea, for the convenience of shipping the produce; the material to be perforated proved to be stone, instead of terrass as was expected, and three hundred and sixty feet in length were accordingly blasted by drilling in

the solid rock, at an expence of about five
thousand pounds currency.

SAINT ANDREW's Parish is the first on the leeward side adjoining the town, it contains four
thousand and ninety-six acres, and the vallies
being narrower, the estates are small and more
compact, neither is it so well supplied with
water, except in Buccament Valley, which is
one of the most extensive and fertile in the
Island. In this parish is the small town of
New Edinburgh, where the depot for the commissariat stores is erected.

SAINT PATRICK is next in order, on the western
coast, containing five thousand four hundred
and twenty-six acres, with the two small towns
of Layou and Barouallie, here the land becomes
much more precipitous and difficult of cultivation, and the fertility decreases, neither are
such of the habitations, as are situated in the
vallies, so salubrious.

The last is SAINT DAVIDS, containing four
thousand one hundred and ninety-eight acres,
whose characteristic features are the same as
the preceding; in Washilabo Valley, and also
at the south point near to the entrance of Chateaubelair Bay, are some fine specimens of

sᴇᴄᴛ. 1. Basaltes; the vicinity of the Souffriere and other lofty mountains ensures the Planters in this quarter plenty of rain, and the facilities of shipping produce, compared with the bold eastern coast are very great, and reduce the expence and risk of an estate considerably. This leeward coast was the first settlement of the French Planters, and Barouallie was the principal town of the Island. There was a Church, which was destroyed in the hurricane of 1780, and has not yet been rebuilt, there are also the remains of a French Chapel near to Chateaubelair, which was blown down at the same time.

Population   The returns of the general Population of the Island are very defective, and have only been taken at distant intervals. By the late census in 1825, the white and free population was four thousand one hundred and twenty-five. Kingstown contains about three thousand persons, the slaves employed in agricultural labour on estates, are nineteen thousand eight *19,863* hundred and sixty-three, and there are about four thousand others employed in other pur- *4,000* suits; such details as exist, will be found in the Appendix No. IV. and V.

The Revenue of the Island is about twenty- SECT. 1.
Revenue. six thousand pounds per annum, and is raised by an annual tax act, by which assessments on all the staple commodities of the Island are made, and a proportionate per centage on the incomes of merchants and other persons, with a poll tax on unattached slaves; Commissioners to carry the act into execution, are named for each parish, and the returns are directed to be given in to the Treasurer in January, from whence the rates are calculated according to the estimated expences of the Island, and submitted to the Assembly.* The Colony derives no pecuniary assistance from Great Britain; the garrison, the proportionate expence of the naval establishment, the packets, and the home salary of the Governor, form the burthen sustained by the mother-country, which is amply compensated by the duties on produce; that on sugar only in 1828, was three hundred and thirty-eight thousand six hundred and twenty-four pounds sterling.†

The gold Coins in circulation are exclusively Coin. Spanish and Portuguese, the Doubloon at the

* See Appendix, No. XIII. and XIV.
† See Appendix, No. XII.

SECT. 1. value of sixteen dollars with the aliquot parts in proportion; the Johannes passes by weight at nine shillings the penny-weight; formerly this coin was the most common throughout the Islands, each Colony mutilating their own by plugs and various marks, to prevent exportation; from these practices the coin became so deteriorated, that in 1818 it was called in at a considerable loss, and Doubloons came into more general circulation. The silver coins are the dollar which passes at ten shillings currency, and Colonial coins of one-fourth, one-eighth and one-sixteenth: the British silver occasionally forms part of the commissariat issues, from which source nearly all the bullion of the country arises, but it is speedily collected by the merchants for remittances to Europe, and is therefore of little benefit as a general circulating medium; the English copper money, and a barbarous Colonial coin, with the equally barbarous names of Stampees and Black Dogs, complete the catalogue. The sterling value of the dollar being four shillings and four pence, gives two hundred and thirty and ten-thirteenths, as the currency value of one hundred pounds sterling. It may be

reasonably expected, since Great Britain has
resumed a metallic currency, and the gold
coinage has of late years been so immense, that
in due time the circulation of it will be extended to the Colonies, by which means an
uniform value will be established through the
Islands, and the abominations of currency will
be removed; this will be productive of the
most substantial benefits, by the reduction of
the exchange to an equitable rate, and consequently the price of such articles as are imported from Great Britain; the Colonial credit
will also be increased from the greater facility
and certainty of remittance. The system has
already been adopted in Tobago, and the French
Islands have always been supplied with their
European coins, which maintain the sterling
value and denomination.

The Garrison for the protection of the Island, Garrison.
since the peace has been reduced to one wing
of a regiment, with a few artillery men, during
the war two regiments were the complement,
which the Government undertook to furnish,
in consideration of the assistance which was
given by the Colony at different periods, towards building the forts and barracks, and of

SECT. 1. maintaining the roads thereto at the public expence.

Militia.　The Militia consists of all the free inhabitants between the ages of eighteen and fifty-five, and is formed into one regiment of five hundred and eighty men, two King's companies of one hundred and fifty men, and two Queen's companies of one hundred and twenty-five men, and twenty-five cavalry, these assemble for exercise once in every month, at different stations in the island. The legislature has endeavoured to keep up an effective force of white persons by requiring the planters to keep one white person for every fifty slaves, under a penalty of fifty pounds for each deficiency.

SECTION II.

Early History—Yellow and Black Caribs—Cession in 1763—Sale of Lands—First War, 1772—Treaty of Peace, 1773—Separate Government—Capture by the French.

THE early history of the lesser colonies in the West Indies is so obscure, and of such little importance in the present age, that it is hardly worthy of any research; there are few records to be found in any writings of those who first visited them, which are not either enveloped in fiction, or distorted by ignorance or prejudice. Imitating the absurd example of the Papal grant of the whole continent of America to the Spanish monarch, other Potentates appear from time to time to have silenced the clamours of their subjects for remuneration, by grants of different islands and tracts of land, with as much propriety, and as little regard for the rights of individuals already in possession of them. Saint Vincent experienced this fate, it is not established that Columbus, or any Spaniards ever were in

SECT. 2. actual possession of this island, the inhabitants were numerous and warlike, the coast was
difficult of access, and the appearance of the
interior was that of a dense forest with numerous rivers and precipitous ravines ; possessing
these natural means of defence, and abounding
with the facilities of existence from a fertile
soil, the ocean and rivers being well supplied
with fish, and the forests teeming with large
trees peculiarly adapted for canoes, it became
a chosen residence for a tribe of natives called
the yellow Caribs ; it was nevertheless included
in the Earl of Carlisle's patent which was
granted by Charles I. in 1627 ; afterwards in
1672, a new commission was granted to Lord
Willoughby, constituting him Governor of
Barbados, Saint Lucia, Saint Vincent, and
Dominica ; on his demise Sir Jonathan Atkins
was appointed, who in 1680, was succeeded by
Sir Richard Dutton.

In 1685, Colonel Edwin Stede was appointed
Lieutenant-Governor ; he seems to have been
the first to assert any actual pretensions to
the Island, as he sent persons to prevent the
French from taking wood and water without
permission, fearing that they might gradually

claim a right of possession from the exercise of SECT. 2. this privilege; notwithstanding this nominal title, the English and French Sovereigns had agreed to an act of neutrality as far back as 1660, which was also confirmed by the Treaty of Aix-la-Chapelle, in 1748. In the occasional visits to Saint Vincent, two distinct races of men were discovered, they were of different origins, and their appearances and manners plainly corresponded with those of different portions of the globe. One of these tribes had evidently descended from the Aborigines * of the Island, those of the other tribe were as evidently intruders, and the great difficulty consists in accounting fairly and fully for their introduction. Probability is the highest species of evidence that has hitherto been attained, and on this foundation the origin of this people rests. Upon a fair comparison, Raynal seems to have given the most satisfactory narrative of the early Settlements of the Europeans

* Baron Humboldt in his Personal Narrative, Vol. VI. p. 9, has given very learned details respecting the tribe of the Yellow Caribs, which it is impossible to abridge into the compass of a note.—See also Bryan Edwards, Vol. I. p. 33, 5th Ed.

SECT. 2. among the natives. When the English and French agreed that Dominica and Saint Vincent should be left to the Caribs as their property, some of these savages who until then had been dispersed, retired into the former, but the greater part into the latter; the population of these children of nature was suddenly increased by a race of Africans, whose origin has never been clearly ascertained; the best opinion is, that about 1675, a ship carrying out negroes from that country for sale, foundered on the coast of Bequia, a small Island near to Saint Vincent, and that the slaves who escaped from the wreck, were received by the inhabitants as brethren. But this was not all, the Proprietors of the Island gave their daughters in marriage to these strangers, and the race which sprang

Yellow and Black Caribs. from this mixture were called Black Caribs, having preserved more of the primitive colour of their fathers, than the lighter hue of their mothers. The Yellow Caribs are of a low stature, the black are tall and stout, and this doubly savage race speak with a degree of vehemence which seems like anger.

At length some difference arose between these two classes, of which the French in Martinico resolved to avail themselves, and thereby to profit by the ruin of both parties; but the smallness of the numbers sent out against them, and the defection of the Yellow Caribs, who refused to supply such dangerous allies with any of the succours which they had promised them, to act against their rivals, and the impossibility of coming up with enemies who kept themselves concealed in the woods, were circumstances which combined to disconcert this rash, and violent enterprize; the invaders who were commanded by Major Paulian were forced to reimbark, after losing many valuable lives, but the triumph of the Black Caribs did not prevent their suing for peace, they even invited the French to come and live with them, swearing sincere friendship; the proposal was accepted, and in the year 1719, many of the French inhabitants of Martinico removed to Saint Vincent. When the French came, they brought their slaves with them to clear and till the ground, the Black Caribs shocked at the idea of resembling persons who were degraded by slavery, and fearing that in process of time,. their own colour, which betrayed their origin, might-be made a pretence for enslaving them,

SECT. 2. took refuge in the thickest part of the woods,
and in order to create and perpetuate a visible
distinction between their race, and the slaves
brought into the Island, and likewise in imita-
tion of the practice of the Yellow Caribs, they
compressed so as to flatten the foreheads of all
their new born infants, and this was thereafter
concluded as a token of their independence.
The next generation thus became as it were, a
new race, they gradually quitted the woods,
erected huts, and formed little communities
on the coast; by degrees they claimed a portion of the territory possessed by the Caribs,
and having learned the use of fire-arms, which
they procured from the French Traders, on
being refused a friendly participation in the
landed property, established themselves as a
separate Tribe, elected a Chief, and again commenced hostilities against the Yellow Caribs;
and by force brought their adversaries to terms
of accommodation, and they ageeed to divide
equally the lands situated on the leeward coast.
It happened however, after this division, that
the Black Caribs experienced a most mortifying disappointment, for most of the new
Planters from Europe, and from the French

Settlements in the West Indies, landed and settled near the Yellow Caribs, where the coast is most accessible. This decided preference occasioned a new War, in which the Yellow Caribs were always defeated, and at length obliged to retire to the windward parts of the Island, some fled to the Continent, and some to Tobago, the few that remained lived separately from the Blacks, who became sole masters of all the lands on the leeward shore, and in the quality of conquerors, obliged the European Planters to re-purchase the lands, for which they had already paid the Yellow Caribs. A Frenchman having produced to a Black Carib Chief a deed of land that he had purchased of a Yellow Carib, was told, he did not know what the paper contained, but pointing to his own arrow, said, if he did not give him the sum he demanded, he would set fire to, and burn down his house that very night.

While these differences were in progress, and while the French were gradually gaining a footing in the Island, George the Ist. granted it to the Duke of Montague, who in 1723, sent out a small armament to take possession, but these new proprietors on their arrival found

SECT. 2. the French influence under the appearance of protection so predominant, and the determination of the Natives to admit no Europeans to a permanent settlement there so fixed, that they were glad to abandon their ill-judged enterprize,* and when the Duke, at a subsequent period endeavoured to establish his claim before the Privy Council, it was disallowed.

Notwithstanding these impediments, the French prevailed by means of continual reinforcements of men and money, and superior skill in agriculture and commercial affairs, so that in less than twenty years, eight hundred whites, and three thousand black slaves, were employed in the cultivation of commodities for exportation, which yielded a sum equal to sixty-three thousand six hundred and twenty-five pounds sterling. The expedition which was sent against Martinico, in 1762, under General Monckton,† and Rear Admiral Rodney

---

* The particulars of this attempt are to be found in Bryan Edwards, Vol. I. p. 410, who transcribed them from a work of Dr. Campbell's, on the Sugar Trade.

† General Monckton was employed in the army under General Wolfe, at Quebec, he obtained a grant of four thousand acres of land in Charlotte Parish, called Monck-

also took this Island; and in 1763, it was
ceded in perpetuity to the British Crown, with- Cession in
out any reservation of the rights of the Caribs, 1763.
and General Robert Melville was appointed
the first Governor.

Upon this Cession, Commissioners were sent
out with the new British Governors, authorising them to sell the Ceded Lands by public
sale, to indemnify the Government for the
heavy expences of the War, and twenty thousand five hundred and thirty-eight acres, were
disposed of for the sum of one hundred and
sixty-two thousand eight hundred and fifty-four
pounds sterling.*

Under this Commission the Lands of French   Sale of
Proprietors purchased of the Caribs originally,   Lands.
and those belonging to the Caribs themselves,
were too indiscriminately sold to British Planters, who came from North America, Barbados

ton's Quarter, which he sold to Messrs. Gemmels and
Baillie for thirty thousand pounds sterling.

* The minimum price fixed was five pounds sterling per
acre, for cleared land, and one pound for wood land, with
sixpence per acre for the expences of the survey; the
terms of payment were twenty per cent down, and the re-
sidue in five years by equal instalments.

and Antigua, to settle here. This severity caused many persons to abandon the Island, but many remained, and for a third time, submitted to purchase their Plantations; but it must be observed, that if the Royal Instructions had been strictly obeyed, the Lands belonging to the Caribs would have been held sacred, notwithstanding the omission in the treaty, for the Instructions strictly enjoined the Commissioners " not to molest them in their Possessions, nor to attempt any survey of their Country, without previous and express orders from Home." The Publication of these Commissions throughout the Island, was but ill relished by the new Settlers, who aimed at nothing less than the Possession of the whole Territory of the Isle; repeated remonstrances were made to the Ministry, complaining of restrictions, and limited boundaries, and a tedious negociation was the result. At length about 1771, soon after the appointment of Brigadier General William Leyborne Leyborne, to be Governor, the Planters resolved to carry into execution their lucrative plans; hitherto cultivation had not extended beyond the river Coubaimarou, but the grant to General Monckton, which commenced from this point, being sect. 2. eagerly bought up by the Planters, and proving to be very fertile Lands, many enterprising persons obtained the sanction of Government for other Grants of Lands beyond that boundary. Attempts were made to take possession of them, which were opposed by the Caribs; this, resistance was construed into a declaration of War, or an act of rebellion against the British Government, and occasioned the commencement of hostilities.

In April 1772, orders were issued from England to send two regiments* from North America, to join such troops as could be spared from the neighbouring Islands, to reduce the Caribs to a due submission, or if that became impracticable through their obstinacy, they were to transport them to such place, as should be deemed by the Governor and Council, most convenient for their reception, and best calculated to secure the tranquillity of the Colony. This expedition was carried on under the direc-

First War, 1772.

* Sir Charles Green, Bart. a General of 1819, was a Lieutenant in the thirty-first, and employed in this service, as was John Simon Farley, a Major-General of 1811, then a Lieutenant in the sixty-eighth.

SECT. 2. tion of Major General Dalrymple, who distinguished himself considerably, on the occasion, yet he was not able before the month of February, 1773, to effect the humiliation of the Caribs. In the mean time an enquiry was set on foot by the opponents of Lord North's Administration, respecting the justice, and propriety of the motives, which gave rise to this expedition, and after a tedious investigation, it was finally resolved, that the measure was founded in injustice, and reflected dishonour on the National Character, a violation of the natural rights of mankind, and totally subversive of that liberty it gloried to defend. This conclusion was productive of immediate orders to suspend hostilities against the Caribs, and to negociate a Treaty with them on reasonable terms. In obedience to these instructions, General Dalrymple made overtures of peace, which were joyfully embraced by the enemy. The following is the substance of the Treaty as appears in the Saint Vincent Gazette of February 27, 1773.

Treaty of Peace, 1773.   ART. I. All hostile proceedings are to cease, and a firm and lasting friendship to succeed.

II. The Caribs shall acknowledge His Ma-

jesty to be the rightful Sovereign of the Island, SECT. 2.
and Domain of St. Vincent, take an oath of
fidelity to him as their King, promise absolute
submission to his will, and lay down their arms.

III. They shall submit themselves to the
laws and obedience of His Majesty's Government, and the Governor shall have power to
enact such further regulations for the public
advantage as shall be convenient. (This Article
only respects their transactions with His Majesty's Subjects, not being Indians, their intercourse and customs with each other in the
Quarter allotted them, not being affected by it.)
And all new regulations are to receive the
approbation of His Majesty's Governor, before
carried into execution.

IV. A portion of the lands hereafter mentioned, shall be allotted for the residence of
the Caribs, from the River Byera to point Espagnole on the one side, and from the River
Auilabou to Espagnole on the other side, according to lines to be drawn by His Majesty's
Surveyors from the sources of the rivers to the
tops of the mountains. The rest of the land
formerly inhabited by the Caribs, for the future
to belong entirely to His Majesty.

SECT. 2.   V. Those lands not to be alienated either by sale, lease, or otherwise, but by persons properly authorised by His Majesty to receive them.

VI. Roads, ports, batteries, and communications shall be made as His Majesty pleases.

VII. No undue intercourse with the French Islands shall be allowed.

VIII. Runaway Slaves in the possession of the Caribs, shall be given up, and endeavours used to discover and apprehend all others, and an engagement shall be entered into, not to encourage, receive or harbour in future any Slaves whatever, a forfeiture of lands shall be the penalty for harbouring them, and carrying them off the Island shall be considered a capital crime.

IX. All persons guilty of capital crimes against the English, are to be delivered up.

X. In time of danger, the Caribs are to be aiding and assisting His Majesty's Subjects against their enemies.

XI. The Three Chains to belong, and remain to His Majesty.

XII. All conspiracies and plots against His Majesty, or His Government, are to be made

known to the Governor, or other civil Magistrate.

XIII. Leave, if required, to be given to the
Caribs to depart this Island with their families
and properties, with assistance in their transportation.

XIV. Free access to the Quarter to be allowed to the Caribs, to be given to persons
properly empowered to go in pursuit of runaway Slaves, and safe conduct allowed them.

XV. Deserters from His Majesty's service,
if any, and runaway Slaves from the French,
to be delivered up, in order that they may be
returned to their Masters.

XVI. The Chiefs of the different Quarters
are to render an account of the names and
numbers of the inhabitants of the several
districts.

XVII. The Chiefs and other Carib inhabitants are to attend the Governor, when required
for His Majesty's service.

XVIII. All possible facility consistent with
the Laws of Great Britain, is to be afforded the
Caribs in the sale of their produce, and in their
Trade to the different British Islands.

XIX. Entire liberty of fishing, as well on the

coast of Saint Vincent, as at the neighbouring Quays to be allowed them.

XX. In all cases where the Caribs conceive themselves injured by His Majesty's Subjects, or other persons, and are desirous of having reference to the Laws, or to the Civil Magistrates, an agent, being one of His Majesty's natural born Subjects, may be employed by themselves, or if more agreeable at His Majesty's cost.

XXI. No Strangers or white persons are to be permitted to settle among the Caribs, without permission obtained in writing from the Governor.

XXII. These Articles subscribed to, and observed, the Caribs are to be pardoned, secured and fixed in their property, according to His Majesty's directions given, and all past offences are to be forgotten.

XXIII. After the signing of this Treaty, should any of the Caribs refuse to observe the conditions of it, they are to be considered and treated as enemies by both parties, and the most effectual means are to be used to reduce them.

XXIV. The Caribs shall take the following

Oath: viz. We A. B. do swear in the name of the immortal God and Christ Jesus, that we will bear true allegiance to His Majesty George III. of Great Britain, France, and Ireland, King, Defender of the Faith, and that we will pay due obedience to the Laws of Great Britain, and the Island of Saint Vincent, and will well and truly observe every Article of the Treaty concluded between His said Majesty and the Caribs, and we do acknowledge that His said Majesty is rightful Lord and Sovereign of all the Island of Saint Vincent, and that the lands held by us the Caribs, are granted through His Majesty's clemency.

(On the part of His Majesty) W. DALRYMPLE.
(On the part of the Caribs)   JEAN BAPTISTE, DUFONT, &c.*

This Treaty discovers an indulgence in Administration towards the Caribs that demanded very different returns from those that they afterwards manifested. The most fertile and beautiful part of the Island was ceded to them in perpetuity, they were enrolled among the

* The British loss on this expedition was one hundred and fifty killed and wounded, one hundred and ten died from disease, and four hundred and twenty-eight were in hospital.

sect. 2. Subjects of Britain, and consequently entitled
to every privilege her constitution could bestow. The Planters adopted a different mode
of conduct towards them from any that they
had hitherto observed, endeavouring by a constant and uniform civility to make them friends,
and to conciliate their esteem.

The Caribs, on the other hand, made professions of perpetuating this infant amity, and
regretted, with apparent contrition, the existence of former feuds. But with what little
sincerity these appearances were put on, the
earliest opportunity demonstrated.

Separate
Govern-
ment.

Hitherto the Island formed a part only of a
Government, which embraced also Grenada,
Tobago and Dominica; but in the year 1776,
these Islands from their increasing importance,
were created into separate Governments, and
Valentine Morris,* Esq. was intrusted with

* Valentine Morris of Piercefield, in the County of Mon-
mouth, Esquire, was entirely ruined by the neglect of the
ministry of that day; the bills which he drew on the Treasury for the use of the Island, were dishonoured by Government, the holders of which prosecuted him, and sold his
considerable estates in England, and the West Indies, and
threw him into the King's Bench Prison. Some of the

the charge of Saint Vincent. From a Narrative of his own Conduct, published by this Gentleman, it appears, that the Island in 1776 was in a deplorable state of distress, and in want of every requisite for its defence. High dissentions subsisted between the Governor and the Inhabitants, the proceedings of the Americans had excited their attention, and alienated the minds of many from their natural allegiance; the Militia Act had just expired, and the Assembly had been dissolved. The Governor with the approbation of the Council, issued a Commission of array, which the Assembly resolved, on the 22d of December, 1778, " to be totally void of legal foundation, and a manifest usurpation on the liberties of the subject," resolving on their part, and recommending the Inhabitants, to arm themselves, and to exert their utmost efforts for the protection of the Island. In the mean time, Lieutenant-Colonel Etherington of the Royal Americans, arrived from Europe with a number of raw recruits, totally unfit for service for the protection of the Colony. But instead of dis-

bills were paid by the Treasury a considerable time afterwards. He died September, 1789.

ciplining his troops, and attending to the state of the fortifications, which had been hitherto shamefully neglected by his predecessors, he kept his men almost constantly employed in felling trees, and clearing an estate on the Wallibo River, about twenty-three miles from Kingstown, which he had obtained, as was alleged by no creditable means, from Chatoyer, a Carib Chief.

At this period, notwithstanding frequent intelligence had reached Governor Morris of the hostile intentions of the enemy, the capture of Dominica, and the arrival of a certain description of persons at Grand Sable, the principal residence of the Caribs on the windward coast, where they were concealed and protected, the ample supply of arms and ammunition from Saint Lucia and Martinico, yet such was the infatuation that pervaded all ranks, and so prevalent was the influence of party, that the general good was totally neglected, and interest and liberty were sacrificed to pique and resentment.

The Count D'Estaing and the Marquis de Bouillé, then at Martinico, obtaining a knowledge of these circumstances, adopted such

measures as might produce the advantages sᴇᴄᴛ. 2.
they wished. A Mons. Du Perier Laroche
was charged with a secret commission to the
Caribs, he accomplished a private landing in
their country, and found them ready to co-
operate with the French against the English,
and to abandon altogether their union with
that power to which, but six years before, they
had sworn allegiance and inviolable attachment. Intelligence however of this business
was communicated to the Governor by Mons.
Gelfrier, a respectable French gentleman, resident in the Island, and the secret emissaries,
although they found means to escape to Martinico, with the news of their success, were
confident that some suspicions were entertained by the English of an impending descent,
so that it became necessary to hasten the expedition, lest the favorable moment should pass
by neglected and unimproved.

On the morning of June the 16th, 1779,
about nine o'clock three sloops of war appeared off Calliaqua without shewing any
colours, and came to an anchor, two in Young's
Bay, and one in a bay rather nearer the capital,
called Warrawarrou Bay. Many of the Plan-

SECT. 2. ters in the neighbourhood were so possessed with the idea of their being merchant ships that were expected from Antigua, to take in sugars, that they absolutely prevented the gunner of Hyde's Point Battery from firing an alarm, though he repeatedly pronounced them enemies; one of them even attempted to go on board, and did not perceive his mistake until it was too late to retire. He was then obliged to surrender himself a prisoner, and attend to the mortifying information, " that they were well informed of the weakness of the situation, and of the dissensions that subsisted in the Colony, that they were in no wise apprehensive of a repulse, as they knew previously to their departure from Martinico, that the key belonging to the magazine at Wilkie's Battery was lost, consequently that they incurred no danger in running down for the harbour; and furthermore, that there was no Militia, and that the principal part of the soldiery were employed by the Colonel in the cultivation of his estate."

During the disembarkation of these troops, Laroche, who had preconcerted the whole of this affair with the Caribs, landed in their country with a few men, and communicated

the watch-word of revolt; they immediately
repaired to his standard with alacrity, and
began to exercise on the English, resident on
their boundary, the most flagrant acts of in-
solence and cruelty; plunder, violence, and
murder marked the first transports of their
career; nor is it to be supposed they would
have altered their conduct, had they not been
checked by their more moderate friends, the
French, who directed their operations.

While Laroche, with about forty-five French,
besides free Negroes and Mulattoes, having
been joined by about six hundred Caribs, awed
and overran the windward part of the country,
and obliged every Englishman to fly from his
abode, the Chevalier Du Rumaine formed his
troops on Sir William Young's Hill, in number
about five hundred, and marched directly towards Kingstown. It appears the Governor's
orders respecting the windward posts were
most shamefully disobeyed by Lieut. Colonel
Etherington; these were, in case the Caribs
remained inactive, to follow any enemy that
should appear off the windward coast, and
passing these posts without attempting to land,
thus coming as a reinforcement, they would

by this manœuvre have placed the enemy between two fires; or in case the Caribs should
stir to assist an enemy, then to attack their
settlements, and thus either to detain or draw
back the Caribs to their own defence; but most
of the troops stationed at the several posts had
been withdrawn by Lieut. Colonel Etherington,
and employed on his estate. Lieut. Gordon
however, although with only half his complement of men, assisted by Mr. James Glasgow,
gallantly defended his post at Colonarie, until
overpowered by superior numbers.

Governor Morris, with a few others were of
opinion that it was possible from Sion Hill,
with one or two pieces of ordnance to keep
the enemy at bay until the arrival of the troops
from the leeward, or perchance the fleet under
Admiral Byron and Barrington, might hear of
the attack, and hasten to succour the Island.
Even with the former an engagement might
be risked with every probability of success, as
the enemy were uncommonly ill appointed,
extremely shabby in appearance, and their resources inadequate to a contest of many days:
according to these conclusions, hasty entrench-
ments were thrown up, some field pieces pointed,

and such measures adopted as must in the exe- cution have operated advantageously. But Lieutenant-Colonel Etherington no sooner saw the French were disposed to advance and attack him, than he censured the resolution of the Governor and his party, as the result of in- experience and temerity; a flag of truce was sent requiring Mons. Canonge, commanding the French troops, to halt until reciprocal pro- posals might be given and received, which was done. Lieutenant-Colonel Etherington even followed the messenger, and brought back de- mands of an unconditional surrender, which were rejected by the Governor;* and after some delay, terms similar to those given to Dominica, were offered and accepted. It is Capture by immaterial to insert these at the present period the French. of time. Considerable misrepresentations were made of the Governor's conduct, arising prin- cipally from the Opposition to His Majesty's Ministry, and from other persons, to screen their own behaviour; so that the Governor applied for, and with much difficulty obtained

* It was commonly said that some *weighty* reasons were produced to the Lieutenant Colonel, which materially di- rected his judgment on this occasion.

SECT. 2. a Court of Inquiry to be held on his conduct, which represented, that in the attack and capture of the Island, he deserved the Royal Approbation, and that of the Country, and that his conduct was not only irreproachable, but meritorious; but of Lieutenant-Colonel Etherington* it was expressed, " That there had been a want of zeal and activity in his conduct, unbecoming an officer; that the military service was carried on by him in a very unsoldierlike and slovenly manner, and that there were sufficient grounds for putting him on his trial;" which was afterwards done in so negligent and discreditable a manner, that the whole business became a mockery.

* This man was originally a drummer; what became of him after the Court-Martial, is not accurately known; he was much indebted on that occasion to the deficiency of memory displayed by one of the witnesses, whose " I dinna recollect," was fully equal to the " non mi ricordo" of modern times : had the Colonel lived in the time of the Wellington school, he would infallibly have been shot or hanged as a coward and a traitor.

SECTION III.

French Government—Restoration of the Island, 1783
—Consequences of the French Revolution—Be-
haviour of the French and Caribs—Insurrection in
1795*—Disastrous Expedition to Windward—Pro-*
ceedings in the Leeward Quarter — Arrival of
Troops — Dorsetshire Hill Stormed — Chatoyer
killed.

GREAT BRITAIN, being engaged in hostilities
with three of the most potent nations in Europe,
and in maintaining her sovereignty in America, did not feel herself in a condition to re-
take the Island, and to indulge those resent-
ments against the Caribs, which she must have
felt, during the four years in which the Island
was under the influence of French politics and
power. The Conquerors however do not appear to have contemplated the permanent possession of the Island. The forms of the British
Constitution remained, the Council and Assembly continued their usual sittings, and the
Writs were issued in the name of the King of
Great Britain. Their general conduct seems

not to have been so laudable, as the few records of this period which remain indicate nothing but acts of oppression, such as arbitrary contributions of money for the payment of the troops, and frequent requisitions of slaves with mules and oxen to labour at the fortifications, for which no compensation was allowed. The French Government also naturally favoured the French Settlers who had obtained leases of lands from the English with certain restrictions imposed on them. To these they granted an amortisement or redemption of the quit rents on payment of the arrears, and a dollar per acre, by which a freehold estate was secured to the purchasers, and the Government realised a considerable sum in specie.

The Marquis de Bouillé was the Governor-General of Martinico at this time, and appears to have conducted himself with such propriety, as to command the esteem and respect of the English in no common degree;* the general

* After the peace the Marquis being in London, some gentlemen interested in West India Property (at the head of whom was that honorable and respected character Drewry Ottley, of Saint Vincent) voted an address of thanks accompanied with a handsome piece of plate, to be presented

officers who were sent as Lieutenant-Governors sect. 3. to Saint Vincent were appointed by him, but of whom little can now be traced. General Du Montet was the first, whose conduct was mild and conciliatory. It was in this year 1780, that the tremendous hurricane took place, which occasioned such dreadful devastation throughout the tropics, and Saint Vincent experienced her full share in the calamity, almost all the dwelling houses, the churches, and other buildings having been destroyed. A gleam of hope shone forth in favour of the English about this time, but it was unhappily of short duration. On Admiral Rodney's return from New York to Saint Lucia, the reports of the ruinous

to him, as a testimony of their veneration and esteem for the humanity, justice, and generosity so exemplarily displayed by him in his several conquests, and chief command of the conquered islands. It was this nobleman, who when thirty-five English seamen were thrown on shore alive from the wreck of the Laurel and Andromeda frigates, on the coast of Martinico, in 1780, took them to his house, and fed and clothed them, and when they were recovered, sent a flag of truce with them to the British officer commanding at St. Lucia, stating that he could not add the horrors of war to those of shipwreck, and he had therefore sent the men free, and at liberty to serve their country.

condition of this captured Island reached him, and with the concurrence of General Vaughan an attempt was made for its recovery; some troops with the Marines were landed in one of the leeward bays, but the difficulties of passage through that part of the country, were found to be insuperable, and the French had established themselves in such force in the forts, that after one day's continuance on shore, the troops were reimbarked, and the enterprise abandoned.

In 1781, Mons. Duplessis superseded General Du Montet; he distinguished himself only by arbitrary demands of money, and supplies for the troops; but in a few months he was relieved by General Blancheland: this officer was greatly respected, and appears not to have merited the tragical fate which awaited him on his return to his native land.* General Freydeau was the next general, and during his administration the French Minister of Marine, by a royal ordinance directed, " les Terres

---

* General Blancheland was appointed Commander-in-Chief at Saint Domingo in 1790, he was sent home as a state prisoner by the Commissioners in 1792, and guillotined at Paris the 17th of April, 1793.

incultes, vagues et non concedes," in Saint Vincent to be granted to Mrs. Martha Swinburne;
the extent of this grant, proves either the utter
ignorance of the Court of Versailles of its newly
acquired possessions, or the powerful influence
of a Dame d'honneur in the Palace, which was
the rank of this Lady, to command so royal a
benefaction. On the Restoration of the Island
in 1786, the British Government considered
these acquired rights as too great an encroach-
ment on the prerogative of the Crown, but,
with characteristic justice, the sum of six thousand five hundred pounds sterling, was voted
to Mrs. Swinburne by Parliament for the purchase of them, and the lands were reconveyed
to his Majesty.* The last French Governor
was the Comte de Tilly, of whom nothing remarkable is recorded: he remained in his appointment during the negotiations of the peace
of Versailles, which was concluded in 1783, Restora-
and on the first day of January 1784, the pos- Island.
session of the Island was restored to the English,

* This extraordinary grant is dated the 9th November,
1782, and recorded in the Secretary's Records, O. 302 ; the
release is dated the 18th of August, 1786, and recorded in
the Register's Book, T. 428.

SECT. 3. Edmund Lincoln, Esq. being appointed Governor.

In March following, the Sessions of the Legislature was opened with a speech recommending many salutary improvements, and
particularly the encouragement of new Settlers
in the room of those, who had abandoned their
attempts at colonization during the prevalence
of war and oppression. The Assembly poured
forth numerous complaints of French exaction
and rapacity, but as lamentations were in vain,
they soon commenced their endeavours to prevent future conquests, by placing the Island
in a state of defence; and they voted five thousand pounds currency, to be expended on the
forts and fortifications, during the ensuing
three years, which unfortunately was only partially accomplished. Governor Lincoln in pur-
suance of the principles recommended by him,
executed a number of grants of land on the
windward coast, but they were received with
distrust and suspicion; the remembrance of
the former disturbances, was impressed on the
minds of the new Settlers, doubts were entertained of the validity of the titles, and cultivation proceeded slowly.

A variety of excesses had been committed by the Caribs against the English during the time the Island was under the French Government, who prudently restrained the sanguinary disposition of their allies, nevertheless their behaviour on all occasions, betrayed their deep rooted enmity and aversion, and occasioned at first a correspondent degree of caution and prudence on the part of the Colonists; but from the evacuation of the Island by the French, to the commencement of the Revolution in Conse-quences of France, the treacherous Caribs, having lost the French their avowed protectors, put on the smoothest Revolution. political exterior, and as early as they could with a good grace, professed themselves enraptured admirers of the mild and benevolent Constitution of Great Britain. And strange as it may appear, notwithstanding past events, they were as successful in imposing on the credulous Inhabitants, as they had been in the former war; and the Planters with all the zeal peculiar to self interest, wished to engage their friendship by every means within their reach. Thus basking in the sunshine of general favour, they were not tempted to forfeit it, but peace and good will were apparent on both sides;

SECT. 3. the Planters extended their cultivation, expensive sugar works were erected, where cotton or tobacco only had been previously ventured to be planted, and the Caribs remained happy and contented within their boundary. Governor Lincoln died in the Government in 1786, and was succeeded by James Seton, Esq. in March 1787.

For some time the Island continued in a state of uninterrupted tranquillity. The commencement of the troubles at Saint Domingo in 1789, appears to have been the first fruits of the French Revolution in the West Indies, and the doctrines of republicanism were gradually diffused through the Islands; these soon reached Martinico, to the annihilation of all order and tranquillity among the inhabitants. Being in the habits of trading thither, the Caribs imported thence those poisoning principles which have since been productive of Behaviour such great changes in the world. In this early of the French and stage of affairs, they discovered nothing further Caribs. than a gloominess of aspect and a reserved behaviour, but this on the defeat of the expedition under Admiral, afterwards Lord Gardner, and General Bruce, in June 1793, against

Martinico, was changed into a haughty and imperious mien, indicating an end to their former wavering and uncertain purposes, and the resoluteness of every future design.

However the success of the succeeding campaign, under Sir Charles Grey, smothered in their infancy any resolutions they might have had in contemplation unfriendly to the interests of the Colony. The reverse of circumstances which ensued on the arrival of Victor Hugues,* at Point a Petre, in the Island of Guadaloupe, in June 1794, and the success of his arms, changed the complexion of their conduct once more, and encouraged them to lay aside in great measure, their borrowed countenances. This infamous revolutionary zealot, bloated with the inhuman, and wide wasting principles of the democratic system, no sooner saw himself in a condition of not only maintaining his

* Victor Hugues was born at Marseilles, and brought up as a Baker; after being Governor of Guadaloupe, he was appointed to Cayenne. On the capture of that settlement in 1809, he went to Paris, where it is said he was obliged to surrender much of his ill-gotten wealth, to prevent inquiries into his atrocious proceedings; he died at Cayenne where he retained some property in 1826.

SECT. 3. new conquests, but also of extending them, than he endeavoured to convert his hopes into certainty by embroiling every Colony in his neighbourhood, and rendering them the theatre of internal war. To accomplish this truly diabolical object, he procured a number of confidential emissaries, whom he instructed to introduce themselves secretly into the English Islands, to sow the seeds of insurrection and revolt, and when they conceived themselves sufficiently entitled, they were to demand a reinforcement, with which he would supply them, and repeat it from time to time as necessity might urge. Those Islands were first attempted where French inhabitants were known to reside, such were Saint Lucia, Grenada, Saint Vincent, and Dominica; in which places the scheme was embraced by many with all the avidity of enthusiasm, especially by the Caribs in Saint Vincent. The agents of Hugues first opened their credentials among their countrymen, and practised on them, and through their medium, on the Caribs; they invited them in the name of the glorious French republic as friends and citizens to accept of liberty and equality, to rouse themselves from

inglorious sloth, and assert the natural prero-
gatives of men; said they, "Behold your chains
forged and imposed by the hands of the tyran-
nical English! Blush, and break those ensigns
of disgrace, spurn them with becoming indignation, rise in a moment, and while we assist
you from motives of the purest philanthrophy
and zeal for the happiness of all nations, fall
on these despots, extirpate them from the
country, and restore yourselves, your wives
and children to the inheritance of your fathers,
whose spirits from the grave will lead on your
ranks, inspire you with fury, and help you to
be avenged."

An address of this kind was grateful to the
prejudices and passions of the Caribs. They
replied, " they were flattered and obliged by
those professions of friendship extended to them
by the French Republic, they were sensible of
their oppressions, and felt uneasy beneath them,
and delayed hostilities on no other account,
but because they wanted a sufficient quantity
of military stores to support the first avowal of
their intentions; on the receipt of these they
would most cheerfully cooperate with their
friends and allies, the Delegates of the Republic,

SECT. 3. in promoting their influence, and the establishment of their own rights." The French
inhabitants who had taken the oath of allegiance to his Britannic Majesty, were the
agents, through whose interference this business reached its present altitude; the first
proposals of Hugues from Guadaloupe, were
instantly adopted as their own, and while in
possession of every immunity, the mild and
benevolent government they were under could
bestow, and sharing the confidence and friendship of their neighbours, they were sinking a
mine pregnant with destruction to blow them
up in an instant. It was finally agreed that
arms and ammunition should be sent from
Guadaloupe as early as possible; that on the
night of the 10th of March, 1795, the Caribs
of the leeward parts of the Island, under the
direction of Chatoyer, and those of the windward, under that of Duvallé, should proceed
to Kingstown, and there unite their forces with
their confederates the French; and that without commiserating either age or sex, they
should, during the hour of tranquillity, massacre all the Whites; they were then to proceed
in all directions throughout the country, and

exterminate every individual composing that
class; mulattoes and black domestics suspected of fidelity to their masters, were included in these instructions.

Fortunately for the Island, the Governor,
James Seton, Esquire, was a man of a cool,
steady, and determined character; he was
materially assisted by his son, of the same
name, who was his Brigade Major, and in the
different military matters which occurred, displayed considerable talent. The cultivation of
the Island had continued to increase, the Sugar
Plantations now extended as far as Byera
River, on the windward coast, and many small
French settlements had been consolidated on
the leeward side; but the state of defence was
very defective, the Garrison consisted of one
serjeant and ten privates of the Royal American
regiment, and one captain, and twenty-seven
artillery men, so that the Colonial Militia was
the only body of men to afford any effectual
resistance, until reinforcements could be obtained from Martinico, then the residence of
the Commander-in-Chief.

A dreadful insurrection having broken out
in Grenada, the President, Keneth M‘Kenzie,

sect. 3. Esq. with commendable zeal, dispatched information of the fact to the neighbouring Islands, which arrived at Saint Vincent on the 5th of March, when the Governor, after advising with his Council, ordered an alarm to be fired; the Militia were immediately under arms, and in the evening appeared on the Parade, where they were reviewed by the Governor, and exhorted to defend themselves with resolution, and render their characters worthy of distinction among their countrymen; assuring them at the same time, that no exertions should be wanting on his part consistent with the duty of the station which he had the honour to fill. It was deemed expedient that a division of the Militia should take place, one half were to remain on their several plantations to maintain order and regularity, and to carry on the management of the estates, the other half were to do duty on Berkshire Hill, during a certain number of days, when they were to be relieved by the former, and so on in rotation; the Queen's company to windward, and the Chateaubelair company to leeward, were excepted in this arrangement; they were left to guard their respective boundaries. Dispatches were sent off to the Commander-in-Chief at Martinico, and every possible exertion made by the inhabitants in the neighbourhood of Berkshire Hill, in carrying up provisions, ammunition, and every thing necessary for the defence of the Colony.

On the following day Mr. William Greig, a merchant, with his family arrived in town from Marriaqua, who informed the Governor and Council, that he had been strongly urged by a neighbouring Carib to withdraw himself from the Island without delay, as it was the unanimous intention of his Countrymen to proclaim war against the English within three days, and that they purposed the extermination of every individual. On the 7th a message was sent to Chatoyer and Duvallé, the two Carib Chiefs residing on the northern extremity of the Island, requiring their attendance upon the Governor and Council on the Tuesday following, according to the 17th Article of the Treaty. This message did not reach them until Sunday morning: their answer was, " it is too late, it might have been sent sooner." On the same Saturday, Mr. Irwin one of the

SECT. 3. Governor's Aides-de-Camp possessing an estate in the Massarica Quarter, was dispatched thither to speak to the Caribs resident within the boundary, upon the subject of this expected Insurrection, and by them to send an order to the Chiefs of Grand Sable, likewise to repair to town on the Tuesday following. The utmost astonishment was expressed by the Caribs at the suspicions entertained against them; they said, " they had been once already deceived by the French, and their misconduct during the late war had been generously cancelled, and since the peace the utmost kindness and humanity had been displayed towards them; no possible advantage could arise by their making war against the English, and no pardon could be expected, should they attempt it; they could not answer for those who resided at Grand Sable and Rabacca, not being in the habits of intimacy with them, but they had received no information from them of any intention to disturb the tranquillity of the Colony." They seemed disinclined to carry any message to the Windward Chiefs, urging in apology the misunderstanding subsisting between them; however, on a considerable

reward being promised they consented. On the
succeeding day, two of those who held this
consultation, returned, observing that they had
seriously revolved in their minds the conference
of yesterday, and, were still of opinion that the
Caribs had no intention of breaking with the
English, but should the generality of them
adopt a measure so absurd, they implored protection for themselves, their wives and families,
as they could not think of rendering themselves
so detestable as to unite against the English,
and after being supplied with refreshments de-
-parted with the utmost apparent cordiality and
good will; and even so late as the 8th of March,
several Gentlemen partook of a Maroon Dinner
within their boundary, with some of the Chiefs.
Yet on the Tuesday following, these very men
were foremost in attacking, plundering and
demolishing the very plantations, where they
had with the greatest apparent sincerity made
these professions, and where they had resided
in ease and affluence for more than ten years.

On Sunday evening in consequence of in- Insurrec-
formation that the Caribs in Marriaqua, which tion in 1795.
is nearer to Kingstown, in conjunction with
the French in that neighbourhood, were com-

SECT. 3. mitting devastations on the estate of Mrs. La
Croix, a French Lady, who with her family,
was considered as well affected to the English,
a detachment of Militia under the command
of Brigade-Major Seton, and a small party of
Volunteers, with some armed Negroes under
Major H. Sharpe, were ordered to apprehend
the perpetrators; late in the night they fell in
with some Carib and French huts, which were
illuminated, and seemed to be the abodes of
cabal and rebellion, men, women and children,
were rioting on the ill-gotten spoils of the day;
Mr. Dupré, a Swiss, was of the English party,
by wearing the national cockade and speaking
the French language, he deceived the conspirators completely, and got undiscovered
among them, but before they could be properly surrounded numbers of them escaped;
only eighteen were made prisoners, many of
whom had in their hats and caps the French
national cockade, and upon searching the
houses, arms and ammunition were found. Yet
still, with respect to open and avowed hostilities on the part of the Caribs, the majority of
the community had taken no active part. On
the 9th of March, James Gerald Morgan, Esq.

the Captain of the Windward Militia, sent
word that he had received intelligence that an
attack was meditated on that part of the country by the whole body of Caribs, and requested
immediate assistance.

Lieutenants Macdowall,* and Hugh Perry
Keane,† were ordered to reinforce him with a
detachment of twenty-two Militia men from
Kingstown, these were joined by twelve Volunteers, and set forward about seven o'clock in
the evening, well mounted, and in high spirits.
Some time in the night they reached the Sans
Souci estate, where they halted until the morning, when it was resolved that the troop should
proceed to the boundary of the Caribs, and
demand a declaration of their intentions; on
reaching Bellevue estate, they were told that
the enemy had already set fire to the dwelling
house on Three Rivers Estate, with the adjoining cane fields, which was soon confirmed by
the ascending smoke and flames.

The troop advanced with all possible dispatch in order to check the progress of the
destroyers, but they were very warmly fired

---

* Daniel Macdowall, Esq. died May, 1829.

† Hugh Perry Keane, a Barrister at Law, died 1821.

upon from the cane pieces. Being in a narrow range of high canes in a valley surrounded by hills on every side, it was thought expedient to retreat until a more advantageous situation could be obtained; but perceiving the number of the enemy to increase every moment, they returned to Captain Morgan's, and joined the detachment under his command. Here it was deliberated what measures were necessary on the occasion, and a variety of circumstances determined them to return to Kingstown without delay; when they had advanced as far as Massarica River, they saw a body of Caribs posted before them, on a ridge which commanded the road; who, on perceiving the detachment halt on their march, took off their hats, and waved them as if inviting them to pass. These appearances imposed so far on some of the party, that they pronounced them friends, and encouraged the rest to go forward; but as soon as the perfidious villains perceived they were completely exposed to their fire, they opened upon them a most tremendous volley of musketry, which they maintained with unabating ardour; it was proposed by some of the party to advance, and charge them; while they were preparing to do this, they were attacked in their rear by another body of the enemy. It was impossible to annoy them in front, as the troops must have ascended a very high bank, and exposed themselves to a fire from the cane pieces around, without the hope of coming near them, for as soon as they fired, they either laid down or ran into the canes; the Caribs were also protected by a large silk-cotton tree, which had been cut down, and answered the purpose of a breast-work. Nothing now remained in this very critical and perilous situation, but to retreat in the best manner possible; accordingly every man effected it as he could, some on horseback, some on foot, with extreme difficulty; many were a long time concealed in the cane fields, and obliged to take circuitous routes to avoid the high roads which were commanded by the enemy, to reach Kingstown.*

In this unsuccessful expedition, thirty-one persons lost their lives, the greatest part of them the most promising young men in the

* One gentleman realized the dramatic incident in Tekeli, concealing himself under a cask, which the sanguinary monsters fortunately passed by unexamined.

SECT. 3. Colony; those who were wounded or made prisoners, received no quarter, but were murdered with every circumstance of savage barbarity; some had their legs and arms cut off, while the living trunks were left writhing in the agonies of pain; others were mangled and cut up in a manner too shocking to relate. This fatal event produced a scene too tragical and melancholy for description. The defeated and disheartened troop, in their precipitate and disorderly flight to Kingstown, communicated terror and dismay as they passed, to all the inhabitants of the Windward Country; the alarm was sudden and irresistible, in a moment both whites and blacks abandoned their abodes, leaving behind them almost every thing they possessed, being no further solicitous than to hasten from the present rapidly approaching ruin. The Caribs inflated with success, and encouraged by the prevaling timidity of all descriptions of people, seemed to invoke the demon of destruction to mark their progress.

No white man was permitted to survive his discovery, even the unarmed and unoffending Negroes were maimed or murdered. All the cane fields and dwelling houses, from their boundary to the River Jambou, and nearly all the sugar works, were set on fire, and many cattle killed on this day; on the following, these ravages were continued as far as Calliaqua, only three miles from Kingstown; on Thursday morning, they reached Dorsetshire Hill, and after pulling down and trampling under foot the British Standard, they displayed in its stead the tri-coloured flag of the French Republic.

While these proceedings were taking place to windward, under the direction of Duvallé, the leeward conspirators under the ruthless and sanguinary Chatoyer (who was Commander-in-Chief) were not less active, though probably from an expectation of acquiring the permanent possession of that part of the country, they did not commit the same devastations that marked the rapid and unvarying progress of the former. Chatoyer had made choice of Mr. Kearton's estate in St. Patrick's Parish, for his share, and consequently no damage was done, either to the works, or even the furniture in the dwelling house, except one cut on a sideboard with a cutlass; this shews their own opinions of the success of this sanguinary enterprize. They

SECT. 3. arrived at Chateaubelair on Tuesday the 10th of March, where they were joined by all the French inhabitants in that neighbourhood, who embarked in the cause with the utmost eagerness and zeal, although some of them afterwards alleged, that they were reluctantly compelled to join the enemy. In a moment they resolved to cancel every obligation they were under for a repeated series of lavish acts of British generosity. On the morning of the commencement of rapine and murder in this neighbourhood, the Caribs made prisoners of three respectable white young men, Duncan Cruikshank, Alexander Grant, and Peter Cruikshank, whom they carried along with them to Dorsetshire Hill. Here they were kept in suspense until the Saturday following, when they were ordered out by Chatoyer, and massacred in the most shocking manner. Great were the exertions of the French and Caribs, while they maintained their position on Dorsetshire Hill; they availed themselves of every possible measure of success and safety within their reach without delay. A supply of provisions and liquors was laid up, being part of the produce of their recent spoils; with infinite labour and

difficulty, they dragged from Stubbs' Bay Battery, two pieces of ordnance, one twelve, and
one four pounder, the latter they got mounted
completely by Saturday night; the heavy piece
lay on the ground loaded with iron, glass, and
stones; at this time their numbers were about
one hundred and fifty whites and coloured
people, and generally from two hundred to
three hundred Caribs.

The conduct of the Governor throughout this
season of distress was most exemplary; on the
earliest intimation of danger, he removed, with
the most valuable and important papers in his
possession, to the Fort on Berkshire Hill, and
proceeded to carry on the necessary fortifications with the utmost assiduity and application;
provision was also made to secure the town,
for the safety of which, the generality of persons were under the most serious apprehensions.
To prevent the enemy from approaching too
near, orders were issued that the surrounding
canes to a certain distance, should be immediately burned; a post was likewise established
on Sion Hill, to block up every accessible
avenue in that direction; a very vigilant and
well attended guard of the militia was main-

tained in the town itself, and on the adjoining estates, armed Negroes were stationed to communicate an alarm on the smallest appearance of danger.

Too great precautions could not have been taken, for the Caribs were frequently seen on Liberty Lodge and Redemption Estates, and once a small party proceeded as far as the Government House, which at this time was on Montrose Estate; none of their positions were six furlongs from Kingstown. During these transactions, Captain Newton of the Artillery, and Major Whytell of the Militia, who maintained the post on Sion Hill, annoyed the enemy considerably, and kept them greatly in awe; at one time they approached so near as to be within reach, when a well directed shot drove them to a greater distance, and they contented themselves with burning the canes on Arno's Vale, and the estates in the vicinity.

Arrival of Troops. The melancholy gloom which overshadowed the Island, was in some degree dissipated on Wednesday morning, by the landing of Captain Campbell,* with a Company of the forty-sixth Regiment from Martinico. On the following

* Dugald Campbell, a Major-General, 1814.

day, the Zebra sloop of war, Captain Skinner,* arrived, and on Saturday His Majesty's ship Roebuck, Captain M'Iver; these reinforcements came very opportunely, as the apparent superiority of the enemy began to shake the fidelity of the Negroes, and to tempt them to abandon the weak and defenceless standard of the Colonists; besides having got their guns in readiness, the French and Caribs waited only for the morning to play upon the camp at Sion Hill, and on the town, from both of which places, a retreat would instantly have been necessary, as Dorsetshire Hill completely commands them. These circumstances, in connexion with others of a similar tendency, rendered it expedient to attempt dislodging them by storm without any further loss of time; accordingly every precaution was taken, and every disposition made by the Governor that could possibly ensure success. On the 14th,

Dorset-
shire Hill
stormed.

---

* Captain Skinner, R. N. was lost in the Lutine Frigate off the coast of Holland, 9th October, 1799. A sword was voted him by the Legislature, but in consequence of his death happening before its presentation, his family requested the vote might be made a silver cup instead of the sword, which was done in 1802.

the party formed at the house of Mr. Hartley, on Sion Hill, at midnight. Captain Skinner of the Zebra, to whom the command was given, led the van with detachments of sailors and marines landed from his own vessel, and the Roebuck; Lieutenants Hill and Groves followed with what sailors could be conveniently collected from the different merchant ships in the bay. The company of the forty-sixth, under Captain Campbell, came next, and Major Whytell and Captain Farquhar Campbell brought up the rear with a number of Militia, and some armed Negroes, in whom they could confide; Major Sharpe was ordered to shew Captain Skinner the road, and inform him of the ground, and Mr. Seymour volunteered as an advanced guide. This brave and gallant little company, with the utmost alacrity received orders to march, and in the preceding order they began to ascend the winding and rugged path, and were enabled to advance within eighty yards of the main post without being perceived. The vigilance of the enemy could no longer be eluded, they were almost at once discovered, challenged, and fired upon; the effects of surprise were hardly perceptible in their manner

of receiving the English, they were immediately
under arms, raised a most tremendous and ap-
palling yell, and came out in great numbers to
sustain the assault, pouring at the same time a
brisk and well continued shower of musketry;
nothing could exceed the intrepidity of the
officers and men on this occasion; they received the enemy's fire without returning a
single shot, until they had approached within
twenty yards of them, when orders were given
to fire a volley and charge; these were instantly obeyed, Captain Skinner and Lieutenant
Hill mounted the bank, and were immediately
followed by the detachment of seamen. Captain Campbell of the forty-sixth, and Major
Leith did the same in another situation; the
buildings in which the enemy sheltered themselves, were stormed, and such of them as made
resistance, were bayonetted; in about fifteen
minutes the fate of the hill was determined,
the enemy fled in all directions, and through
the darkness of the night, many of them effected their escape. In this attack five seamen
were killed, and Lieutenant Hill and four men
wounded. On the side of the enemy, several
of the French and Caribs lay dead on the field, Chatoyer killed.

among the latter was Chatoyer, the Commander-in-Chief of all the forces. Cruelty rather than courage had always been the principle of this man's conduct, he therefore fell unregretted in single combat with the brave Major Leith of the Militia; there was found upon him a silver gorget, given to him by His present Majesty, then Prince William Henry, on a visit to Saint Vincent, during the Prince's cruise on the West India Station.

This blow was not more unexpected than effectual, the French were instantly panic struck, and despairing of any further success, no longer united with the Caribs; on the contrary, they in general forsook them, and endeavoured with the utmost possible secrecy and celerity, to reach Layou, a town on the leeward coast, about eight miles distant, from whence it is supposed they either meditated an escape, or flattered themselves it was practicable to impose on the credulous English once more, by affecting a neutrality. However they were unsuccessful in their retreat, for the Negroes who still remained on the plantations through which they were obliged to pass, being apprised of their defeat, lay lurking for their prey, and

intercepted great numbers, among whom was
the Secretary of the Conspiracy, Mons. Dumont.
These distinguished champions of equality a
few days after their apprehension, were most
deservedly hanged, and their bodies towed out
beyond the harbour, and committed to the
flood ; for the same cause a similar sentence
was executed on about twenty others, who were
found in arms, after having taken the Oath of
Allegiance. The Caribs in the mean time were
not less alarmed, the fate of Chatoyer was
severely felt by every individual among them,
and their boldness and intrepidity evidently
forsook them. Confounded and dismayed, they
retreated to their own country, wishing no
doubt that they had never commenced the undertaking. Had there been troops sufficient
to have pursued this advantage, a rapidity of
success in all probability would have ensued,
and the destruction of the enemy have been
accomplished without delay ; but the colonial
resources were so inadequate, that the attempt
was wholly impracticable. It was however
conceived that some good effects might result
from arming such Negroes as might be de-
pended on, and sending them in pursuit of the

SECT. 3. fugitives, with orders to kill or make prisoners of as many as possible; but it was soon discovered that expeditions of this kind did not tend to promote the general good, or to restore tranquillity to the Colony; they were marked with cruelty, hurried on with disorder, and inspired by rapacity, and many innocent persons lost their lives.

The Governor and Council therefore prohibited them in future, unless carried on with greater uniformity, and so directed as to facilitate the wished for end.

SECTION IV.

Post at Chateaubelair — Proclamation — Calliaqua burnt—Arrival of the forty-sixth Regiment—Attack —A Camp at Calliaqua—Rangers formed—Duvallé's Settlement taken—The Caribs at the Vigie— Attack on Calliaqua—Dorsetshire Hill taken and retaken—Reinforcement arrived—Movement on the Vigie—Enemy driven from the Vigie.

In the leeward quarter, on the 18th, Colonel Gordon* marched to Chateaubelair with a detachment of the Northern Regiment; by his prudence and activity, he kept the enemy from any attempt in that neighbourhood, and effectually protected all the estates upwards, from the plunder they had hitherto been exposed to from the Negroes, and small parties of French and Caribs; he continued to keep his post, and by judicious and well conducted excursions took a considerable number of prisoners, it became necessary notwithstanding to burn the Town of Chateaubelair. The enemy destroyed the upper works, and the canes on Wallibo

* Robert Gordon, President of the Council, died September 1829, at the advanced age of ninety-one years.

SECT. 4. estate, and murdered Mr. Grant the Overseer, by inhumanly passing his body between the cylinders of the sugar-mill. But comparatively, the leeward Planters might be called fortunate, with those on the windward side.

Proclamation. The Governor published a very spirited Proclamation, dated the 20th of March, in which he enumerated the barbarities and unjustifiable conduct of the enemy, and declared, " That he was bound to consider the attack as a treasonable plot, not conducted for the fair and avowed object of conquest, but for the purpose of exterminating the English Inhabitants of the Colony; to such an enemy he could not allow the laws of war, they had begun the violation of them, and professed to hold them in contempt; to those who might come against us as an open and avowed enemy, and who by the fortune of war might fall into our hands, he promised the same treatment, which our Countrymen who were prisoners received from them; also, he promised protection to the French Inhabitants who remained faithful to the Oath of Allegiance which they had taken, and he allowed a period of five days for those who had been seduced from their duty, to

surrender themselves, excepting of course those
who had been concerned in any of the murders
committed, or who had been principals in this
unnatural Rebellion."

The latter part of this Proclamation had no
effect, as all were too deeply committed to derive advantage from it, but it developed the
intentions of the Governor, of whom it is but
justice to say, that he resolutely carried them
into effect, as long as circumstances required
such determined conduct.

In a short time the Caribs had in some degree recovered their panic, and began to shew
themselves in the neighbourhood of Calliaqua.
They soon formed three camps contiguously
pitched between it and the high ground, about
three miles distant from the British encampment on Sion Hill; from these strong holds
they were seen to issue every day in small and
various parties, and to range the ruined and
depopulated country, sometimes to forage, at
other times to reconnoitre. On the 21st the Calliaqua
most valuable part of the town of Calliaqua burnt.
was burnt, and once they were so daringly re-
solute at mid-day, in defiance of the guns, as
to advance to the very base of Sion Hill, and

SECT. 4. to set fire to the sugar works on Arno's Vale estate, which were totally consumed in a few hours; the Villa, Belmont, and Fairhall Estates shared the like fate, and many defenceless Negroes were barbarously murdered.

The fleet which had been so long and anxiously expected, was reported to have arrived at Barbados on the 30th of March; the receipt of this news was diffusive of general joy; but owing to some delay, no assistance reached the Island before the 5th of April, when Arrival of two transports arrived from Martinico, under the 46th Regiment. convoy of the Montagu seventy-four, with the forty-sixth regiment, which was landed the next morning; the soldiers marched immediately to Berkshire Hill, their appointed quarters. The troops were landed under every possible advantage. Three years residence in Gibraltar had prepared them for the climate in which they were to act; they were apparently in the highest health and discipline, and shouts and acclamations from all descriptions of society, hailed them on their arrival. On the 8th, the ship Cockran, Wiseman, arrived from Liverpool, and not observing the ruined state of the country, put nine seamen on shore at

Greatheed's Bay, to prevent their being pressed. They were immediately descried by the Caribs from their camp, and a large party marched down, and surrounded them; a party from Sion Hill pushed after them, but were unable to effect a rescue; it being feared that similar cases might occur, and it being also judged expedient to establish a post at Calliaqua to prevent succours being thrown in to the enemy, an attack on their camp was determined by the Governor. On the 10th the necessary dispositions were made, Captain Campbell of the forty-sixth, at the head of the Grenadiers, was to make the attack. In case of success, Captain Hall* with the Light Infantry was to intercept the enemy's retreat to Calliaqua in one direction, and Colonel Lowman of the Militia with his men, and a detachment of sailors from on board the Roebuck, was to perform the same services in another. Agreeably to this plan of operations, the different parties marched for their respective destinations, about ten o'clock at night, and reached them about one in the morning. It is conjectured that the Attack. enemy had early and accurate information of

* John Hall, a Major-General in 1813.

G

SECT. 4. what was going forward; the extraordinary
vigilance of their sentinels, and the spirited reception of the troops justify the supposition,
for hardly had the Light Infantry stationed
themselves, before they were discovered, challenged, and fired upon, the compliment was
instantly returned, and a very smart engagement commenced; but from the superior number of the attacked, and the damage sustained
by the arms of the men in marching through
heavy and successive rains, the English were
obliged for some moments to fall back, or at
least hesitate in the assault. During this in-
terchange of hostilities, Colonel Lowman, with
the Militia and sailors, was within a short distance of their intended position, when the word
of retreat was given unnecessarily, and unex-
pectedly, by some unknown person in the advanced files; a sudden and invincible panic
seems to have pervaded all the ranks, disorder
and confusion succeeded, the van fell back
upon the rear with such impetuosity, that many
were thrown down and trampled upon; nor
did they conceive themselves secure until they
had regained Kingstown, which they accomplished early the next morning; the retreat of

the Light Company was but of short duration, they were opportunely supported by Captain Campbell, who that moment came up with the Grenadiers of the forty-sixth, and by Lieutenant Farquharson with twenty-two men of the third battalion of the sixtieth; the whole charged the enemy with such determined bravery, that nothing could withstand them, and they fled on all sides with the utmost precipitation. The loss of the enemy was considerable, but as the Caribs generally carry off their dead, not more than twenty were found; the English loss was two killed, and a few wounded of the regulars. Of the Volunteer Militia, which, under Captain William Fraser, behaved with great spirit, Messrs. Thomas B. Taylor, Philip Hepburn, and John M'Broom were killed, and Alexander Stewart* and Joseph Richardson wounded; the three persons killed were much lamented, and the following day were interred with military honours. Their loss was in a small measure compensated for by the recovery of the sailors, who had been taken prisoners,

* Alexander Stewart, a Surgeon resident at Layou, receives a pension of £100. currency from the Colony.

SECT. 4. the enemy not having put them to death immediately according to their usual custom.

After the troops had taken some necessary
refreshment, and demolished the different en-
campments of the enemy; they proceeded
immediately to the barrack ground, above
Camp at Calliaqua, where they intrenched themselves,
Calliaqua.
and in some degree set limits to the depreda-
tions and excesses of the savage and barbarous
foe.

These successes inspired the Colonists with
the hope of obtaining more, and conceiving
that reinforcements were necessary to carry on
operations with energy, a temporary suspension
took place; to procure these reinforcements, it
was determined to arm a proportion of Slaves
on every estate throughout the Island. Each
Negroe on receiving arms was to be appraised,
and in case any mischance befel him during
the period of his military services, the Colony
became amenable to his owner for the amount
Rangers of his appraisement. Five hundred were im-
formed.
mediately put in requisition, and in a few days
were produced on parade, Brigade Major Seton
was named as their Lieutenant-Colonel, the

other officers were appointed out of the different sect. 4. regiments of Militia, and a Serjeant from the Regulars was appointed to each company. They very soon became a most useful and active body of men.*

The settlement of Duvallé, the Carib chief, situated at the northern extremity of the Island, was considered as a proper object of an expedition, as well to divide the force of the enemy, as to annoy them. On Saturday the

---

* The names of the officers composing this corps were,

Lieut.-Colonel.	Lieutenants.	Ensigns.
* James Seton.†	Thomas Slater.	M'Duff Fyfe.†
Major.	Robert Lauder.	W. B. Tanye.
Alexander Leith.	Robert Douglas.†	John Cruikshank.
Captains.	Warner Ottley.†	John Smith.
Andrew Ross.	Alex. Cruikshank.†	Robert Oliver.
William Fraser.	James Riddoch.	
William Alves.	Hubert Jennings.	
John Gordon.†	David Kelly.	
	Thomas Patterson.	
	George Hartley.†	

---

* In 1798, the planters and merchants entered into a subscription, and presented Lieutenant-Colonel Seton with a piece of plate and a sword, of the value of three hundred guineas.

† Officers living.

SECT. 4. 25th of April, two armed Schooners sailed from Kingstown with the following troops on board under the command of Lieutenant-Colonel Seton, who was to direct the operations of the attack, one Serjeant and three Privates of the Royal Artillery, Lieutenant Groves with thirty-three sailors belonging to the Roebuck, and two Lieutenants, one Ensign, five Serjeants, and sixty-four rank and file of the Rangers, as the black corps before mentioned was named, they were reinforced at Chateaubelair, with a small detachment of the forty-sixth regiment, commanded by Ensign Lee. Early in the morning of the 26th, they sailed for the destined scene of action, and attempted a landing in the rear of the houses, and of some batteries which looked toward the sea; but owing to the ignorance of the guides, it was found impracticable to ascend the rugged acclivity in that direction, as they could not discover any vestiges of a path. Lieutenant-Colonel Seton instantly reconnoitered the situation, and saw that it was impossible to make the attack in any other place, than in front of the houses and batteries; therefore under cover of the armed vessels, though exposed to the incessant fire of grape shot, and small arms from the enemy, they effected a landing, and without the loss of a moment, formed themselves beneath the shelter of a cliff. Now the storming of the batteries became the main object, and their gallant commander led them on with uncommon order and intrepidity; the path by which they ascended was angular, consequently they must have been frequently liable to flanking from the swivels placed at certain angles; in addition to this, numbers of massy rocks were precipitated upon them from on high, very much to their annoyance; however from their brave perseverance, every opposition was surmounted, and victory was obtained; twenty- Duvallé's five houses were devoted to the flames, vast Settlement taken. quantities of provisions were also destroyed; but what must have rendered the defeat doubly formidable, was the loss of sixteen canoes, and four swivels, which were found on the batteries. The English loss was three seamen killed, one wounded, three rank and file of the forty-sixth, and six Rangers wounded; the loss of the enemy could not be ascertained, as they carried off their killed and wounded.

During these transactions, the Brigands who

SECT. 4. had survived the storming of the three camps
on the 10th of April, together with the Mariaqua and Windward Caribs, and those English
Caribs at and French Negroes who joined them, as-
the Vigie. sembled on the Vigie, and commenced throwing up fortifications, which in a few weeks
appeared from Dorsetshire Hill (the distance
in a direct line is about four miles) regularly
designed, and otherwise respectable. On the 7th
of May, about nine o'clock in the morning, the
appearance of the enemy was rather alarming,
from their numbers, and several of them being
armed with remarkably long pikes, little doubt
was entertained of their having received a rein-
Attack on forcement. About eight hundred as was sup-
Calliaqua. posed, appeared descending the hills in eight
distinct columns, directing their course towards
the camp at Calliaqua, then maintained by the
Honble. Captain Molesworth* of the forty-
sixth, with one hundred Regulars, and nearly
as many Rangers. On their advancing within
range of the guns, a six pounder was discharged

* William John, sixth Viscount Molesworth, became
Major-General, and Lieutenant-Colonel of the ninth foot;
he was lost in the Arniston Transport off Lagullas Reef on
his passage from Ceylon, May 1815.

upon them, which occasioned their halting. After reconnoitering the camp, and deliberating some small space of time, they beat a parley, and sent in a flag of truce, which was borne by a young French officer, he said, " He was instructed by the General commanding yonder national troops, to desire the British Commander to surrender himself, and his men, prisoners for the time being; they should in consequence be transported to any other English Island, where the flag of liberty was not unfurled, but they could not be permitted by any means to remain in Saint Vincent, his agreeing to this proposal, would entitle him to indulgence, his refusal, provoke an immediate assault, the consequences of which he could not be answerable for." These conditions of capitulation were received by Captain Molesworth, as they deserved, with the utmost contempt; he replied, " that he could depend upon his men, that he did not despair of defending himself, and would do so to the last extremity, having therefore taken this resolution, he would not listen to any proposal derogatory to the character of a British Officer." With this answer the flag departed, but returned again in

SECT. 4. less than an hour, and exultingly remarking on
Captain Molesworth's temerity, exhorted him
not to provoke an attack, as he was too feeble
to resist, observing that he came to make the
last overture he was to expect, namely, " That
he was permitted to march to Kingstown unmolested, provided he laid down his arms, and
left the camp as it then was, with all the ammunition and military stores it contained."
This message was as ill-fated as its predecessor,
Captain Molesworth bravely refusing to comply.
In case he had consented to deliver up his
arms, and march from the encampment, the
troops of the Republic would have received
them, and marched in; all this would have
been perfectly consistent with the terms proposed and accepted, but in the mean time, their
allies the Caribs, had concealed themselves in
the mill and Negroe-houses of the Villa Estate,
near to which they were to pass on their way
to Kingstown, where not one of them would
ever have arrived: unarmed and unprotected,
they must have fallen victims to the savage
cruelty of a concealed foe ; but the steady and
determined conduct of the British Commander
totally defeated their expectations, and pre-

vented those consequences, to which through their inhuman stratagems, both he and his little army would have been inevitably exposed.

While the above negociations were on foot, the Alarm Frigate appeared in sight, on the earliest intimation of the enemy's descent from the Vigie, she got under weigh in Kingstown Harbour, and stood for Calliaqua. In less than an hour she came to an anchor contiguous to the camp, and poured a whole broadside upon the foe, with such well directed aim, that it was said to have done considerable execution among them; on her repetition of the discharge, and landing one hundred and thirty sailors, they scampered away with the utmost expedition, apparently disposed to return to the Vigie. During this transaction, a detachment of the Regulars, and another of the Militia and Rangers, with a six pound field-piece under Captain Hall, were ordered to take post on Dorsetshire Hill, to secure more effectually the safety of the town. About one o'clock the next morning the out-posts were attacked with an impetuosity superior to any thing that had ever been experienced from the Caribs; the fact is that not one of them was concerned.

SECT. 4. The onset owed its vigour to the united efforts of the French Troops lately arrived, and the disaffected Negroes and Mulattoes of the Island, they advanced from Orange Grove about three hundred in number, after a brave resistance of about an hour, their ammunition being expended, the English Troops were obliged to retire, leaving the enemy in possession of the hill, together with the gun; they were not however suffered long to retain their conquest, for the Governor on perceiving that the post was attacked, immediately ordered a body of Regulars, Militia and Rangers, amounting to two hundred men to gain the heights by Orange Grove; the Regulars were led by Captain Foster, the Militia by Major Whytell, and the Rangers by Major Leith, the whole under the direction of Lieutenant-Colonel Seton, and at day break this party had gained those heights unperceived by the enemy; they instantly pushed on, and after a short, but sharp conflict, the enemy fled on all sides, leaving a considerable number of their pikes behind them, they were pursued and several taken or killed who had concealed themselves in the bushes about the hill; forty-eight were killed, nineteen of whom were

Dorset-shire Hill taken,

and re-taken.

whites, and five were taken prisoners, the English loss was nine killed, and twenty-six wounded, those of the Militia killed, were Messrs. Seymour, Weir, Howard and Gillies. It appeared from the examination of the prisoners that the enemy had received a reinforcement of one hundred and ten men from Guadaloupe, of which about forty were white persons. It having been deemed expedient to contract the limits of defence, the post at Calliaqua was withdrawn.

When the defeated enemy reached the Vigie, they began to fortify and strengthen it still more, with the most unwearied diligence. For the purposes of an encampment, nature had been peculiarly friendly to the situation they had chosen, the hill itself was about one hundred yards in length, and twenty in breadth, bounded almost wholly by vallies hardly passable, this was maintained as the citadel, or dernier resort, and was barricaded all round with sugar hogsheads filled with earth, these they had collected from the different dismantled plantations which had been subject to their ravages; within musket shot towards the north-west point, another little conical hill rose to a sect. 4. considerable height, which became their first redoubt, and promised to be very serviceable, as it rendered difficult any approaches to the main position, in the direction which was easiest of access. About cannon shot nearly the same way, rose another hill, which overlooked the road coming from Kingstown in the most commanding manner. This was their advanced post or outward picket guard. During these defensive positions on their side, the necessary fortifications on Dorsetshire Hill, were carrying on, in order to secure its future possession. About this period the Caribs seemed delighted with every opportunity of slaughter and devastation, hitherto they had carried themselves towards the Negroes in a very wily and politic manner, they had offered them liberty, and exhorted them to receive it; but, happily for the inhabitants, the proposal, however flattering, was rejected with disdain, comparatively very few espoused their interests, while a considerable number opposed them well armed, and either gallantly fell, or triumphed, with their masters. In consequence of this inflexibility of conduct in the Negroes, they became equally the objects of detestation with their owners, immediate death was inflicted on all who fell into the hands of the Caribs; the great scarcity of provisions which prevailed among the numbers pent up in town, impelled them to adventure beyond the lines to search for subsistence, these excursions of necessity proved fatal to many, as numbers were taken and destroyed.

General Sir John Vaughan having visited this Island on the 30th of May, and inspected the posts, on his return to Martinico, where he held the chief command, that Island being the head quarters, sent over a reinforcement of Artillery and a quantity of stores, these were followed by a detachment of Major Malcom's * corps of Rangers, consisting of one hundred men, on the 8th of June, and on the ensuing day the third battalion of the sixtieth, consisting of six hundred men, well appointed, and under the command of the gallant Lieutenant-Colonel Ritchie, also arrived; with these reinforce-

* Major Malcolm was an excellent Officer, he had distinguished himself at Martinico by training the Militia, and acquired the esteem of all; he was killed at Saint Lucia in an attack on the battery of Secke, close to the works of Morne Fortunée, April 1796.

SECT. 4. ments, the views of the Colonists, were instantly
turned towards the enemy. Two days were occupied in making the necessary arrangements
and dispositions. On the 11th of June, the
Movement troops received orders to march that evening,
on the
Vigie. at different periods, and in different divisions.
Lieutenant-Colonel Leighton's* division consisting of a part of the fortieth regiment, a party
of Rangers under Captain Gordon, a detachment of Artillery, and seamen from the merchant ships, with four six pounders, and two
small mortars, under Captain Newton, moved
from Sion Hill about eleven o'clock, and proceeded without interruption through the Town
of Calliaqua, and along Belmont Road, to
within pistol shot of the dwelling house, where
they arrived about two o'clock, and halted.
Lieutenant-Colonel Ritchie's division, which
consisted of part of the third and fourth bat-
talions of the sixtieth✝ regiment, upwards of
seventy Militia under Major Whytell, and
Major Malcolm's corps of Rangers, moved

* Sir Baldwin Leighton, Bart. a General in 1819, died in
1828.

✝ Jacob Tonson, Lieutenant-Colonel, 1812, was a Lieutenant in this service.

from Sion Hill about two o'clock, proceeded
up Warrawarou Valley, as far as the works on
the Fountain Estate, and then took the route
of the Vigie road. The corps of Rangers commanded by Lieutenant-Colonel Seton, with a
strong detachment of the sixtieth, under Lieutenant-Colonel Prevost,* having a greater distance to march, moved earlier in the evening
than the two preceding divisions, they proceeded along the high road until they arrived
at that leading to Calder Works, up which
they marched until they reached Calder Ridge,
when they divided. Major Ecuyer of the sixtieth, and Major Leith of the Rangers, with a
party of both these corps, marched to Augustine's Ridge, at the head of Biabou Valley.
Captain Martin of the sixtieth, and Captain
Fraser of the Rangers, took post on the bridge
at the Curreer Estate in Mariaqua Valley:
Lieutenant-Colonel Seton of the Rangers, and
Lieutenant Brown of the sixtieth, took post at
the Jambou Pass, near to the Mesopotamia

---

* Sir George Prevost, Lieutenant-General, died January
1816, he was Governor of Dominica in 1803, and afterwards of Halifax; his last appointment was Governor-
General of Canada.

H

Works; Lieutenant-Colonel Prevost of the sixtieth, and Captain Alves of the Rangers, remained at Calder Ridge; these positions were taken to cut off the retreat of the enemy.

About day-break, Lieutenant-Colonel Ritchie's division began the attack on the upper post of the enemy, which was occupied by about two hundred and fifty Caribs, from which they immediately fled down to Mariaqua after the first fire; the division then pushed on to the second height, which was also soon abandoned. The enemy at first only observing this division, actually came out to attack it; but Lieutenant-Colonel Leighton appearing at that instant, they precipitately returned: a like sortie was attempted on Lieutenant-Colonel Prevost's party, but after advancing two hundred yards, the enemy likewise returned; the Grenadiers of the forty-sixth as soon as the firing began, climbed through the brushwood on Belmont Ridge, and pushed on to support Lieutenant-Colonel Ritchie and the Light Company, keeping the road until it rose upon the ridge, met the Grenadiers, and they advanced together. The guns kept the road until they arrived at the upper end, where the enemy had cut a deep trench across; but this impediment was soon surmounted by the exertions of the Artillerymen and Sailors, who lifted the guns up a steep bank, upon the Ridge; the mortars were got up in the like manner, and opened on the enemy as soon as they were lifted up. Two of the guns were moved on through a very severe fire, until they arrived at a position near the second height, where they opened at a very short distance. The troops under cover of the second height, kept up a constant and heavy fire on the enemy, which was returned with great spirit, but more particularly against the Artillery; but the shot necessary to supply the great guns became expended, and most of those who were acquainted with their management, were either killed or wounded; in consequence of this change of circumstances, their resistance gradually diminished, until about eight o'clock they found it expedient to beat the chamade, which occasioned a momentary suspension of hostilities on the part of the English, when a flag of truce was sent, which proposed, " An immediate evacuation of the Vigie, with all its stores and furniture, provided they might be permitted to bury the dead, and march with

SECT. 4. their troops, carrying their arms and wounded with them unmolested, to the Carib country." Colonel Leighton replied, " He would not admit of any conditions whatever; that the French General must make a discretionary surrender, and rely on the British clemency." During this interval of negociation, the enemy endeavoured to steal away unperceived; the object of it was only to amuse and gain time: a party of the forty-sixth were ordered to storm the place, which they did, followed by the whole; only a few of the national troops tarried to receive mercy, the rest dashed through all manner of danger, like men wholly influenced by despair, and in consequence of this temerity, numbers perished; thus escaping captivity, and perhaps the ignominy of execution, which was the justly awarded punishment of every inhabitant carrying arms. The whole of the Caribs retired very early in the morning, and by that means principally escaped through Mariaqua before the destined parties had been able to arrive at their respective posts. In the place were found three four-pounders mounted on field carriages, and sixteen swivels, some mounted, others lying on the ground; they did

Enemy driven from the Vigie.

not appear to have any round shot for their SECT. 4.
guns, but supplied their place with mill-wedges,
cooper's rivets, cart wheel nails, long stripes of
lead tied in bundles, and every other rascally
substitute they could invent. Twenty-three of
the enemy were found killed in the forts, of
whom sixteen were Whites, and about sixty
were taken prisoners, among whom was Mons.
Souhallet* the Commander, with five French-
men, and four Whites belonging to the Island,
the rest were free coloured people and Negroes.
Lieutenant-Colonel Prevost intercepted and
killed many of the fugitives in their retreat
through the Calder Estate, and not a fourth
part of the whole escaped : the British loss was
in officers, one killed and three wounded, and
thirteen privates killed, and fifty-five wounded.
Captain Piquet of the third battalion of the
sixtieth, was the officer killed, and Thomas
Clapham, Joseph Preston, with Thomas Taylor,
a free coloured person, those of the Militia.

---

* This officer behaved with most distinguished courage
and skill, but he was so infected with revolutionary principles, as to have lost sight of those qualities which dignify
man ; he was too sullen and ferocious to command esteem ;
his loss was severely felt by the enemy, whom he had inspired with unusual confidence.

SECTION V.

*Caribs Retreat to Mount Young—Post at Owia—
Escape of the Caribs—Their Camp at Wallibo—
Reinforcement from Saint Lucia—Lafond's Hill—
Skirmishes at Morne a Garou and Musements—
Attack at Morne Ronde—General Myers arrived—
Owia taken—Attack and Retreat from the Vigie
—Evacuated by the Enemy.*

THE different parties that had taken post in
Mariaqua, were employed after the affair of
the Vigie was over, in scouring that valley,
and destroying the houses of the enemy; some
were killed, and others taken prisoners, but
the troops met with some opposition from
Augustine's party at his Ridge, where a few
men were wounded, from imprudently exposing
themselves; before night however, Mariaqua
was cleared of the enemy, the Caribs retreating
to Massarica. Lieutenant-Colonels Leighton
and Ritchie marched from the Vigie in the
afternoon, after leaving at that post Captain
Campbell of the forty-sixth, with a detachment
of that regiment: they took the route to

Mariaqua, and joined the other corps at the Works on Curreer, where the whole halted that night except Lieutenant-Colonel Prevost's party, which took post at Calder Mill, and Major Ecuyer's, which remained all night upon Augustine's Ridge. On the morning of the 13th, the whole began their march to the Windward Quarter; Lieutenant-Colonel Leighton, with the principal body proceeding up the Valley of Mariaqua, and joining Major Ecuyer, marched down Biabou Valley, falling into the high road at the Adelphi Estate; the remaining parties gained the high road in different directions by Jambou River, and the Calder Road, together with the Artillery; and the whole joined and encamped near the ruins of the dwelling house on the Union Estate, where they remained waiting for provisions, until the 15th, on which morning the troops again marched, and arrived at Bellevue Ridge early in the afternoon. There they halted until the next morning, and then moved on towards Mount Young, which they reached in a few hours, without any loss from the enemy, who made no opposition worthy of notice; but seven men died from the fatigues of the march.

SECT. 5. The enemy made their appearance upon different ridges, but constantly retreated on the
approach of the troops.

The Caribs fled so precipitately from Mount
Young, as to leave all their houses standing,
from which fortunate circumstance, the troops
found sufficient shelter from the weather; great
quantities of corn were found in their houses.
No time was lost after gaining possession of
Mount Young, in destroying the enemy's petit
augres, canoes and houses at Grand Sable,
some of the vessels were so large as to be stiled
" their men of War," about two hundred were
destroyed. In this service the corps of Rangers
were particularly employed, and proved very
active and useful; many Negroes also were
employed in digging up and destroying the
provisions of the enemy, under cover of the
troops. Alexander Wiseman, a Volunteer in
the forty-sixth, was killed by the accidental
discharge of a musket.

Post at
Owia.

It being deemed expedient to occupy the
old post at Owia, which is situated on a pro-
montory at the north-east point of the island,
as well to prevent any succours being thrown
in there, as in time to cooperate with the

troops from Mount Young. On the 23d of June, detachments from the forty-sixth and sixtieth regiments, with Malcolm's Rangers, under the command of Major Ecuyer, sailed for that place, in two Droghers, under convoy of the Thorn Sloop of War, and arrived on the 25th. In their first attempt to land, the boats were obliged to return to the vessels, after having nearly reached the shore, from a heavy fire which was opened upon them by the enemy from a four pounder, and two wall-pieces, concealed in the bushes, and behind the old walls which killed and wounded several of the troops. A smart fire from the vessels however soon drove them off, and the party at length landed, and established their post without any further opposition. Several skirmishes ensued with this party, and that at Mount Young, in one of which, Captain Schneider of the sixtieth was killed.

The possession of this landing place at Owia gave a decided advantage over the enemy, they could not calculate on any external resource, as all the bays were in the possession of the English ; their internal supplies could not hold out many weeks, their own consumption was

SECT. 5. considerable, and that of the troops at Mount Young was immense; great difficulties were experienced in procuring these, and much dissatisfaction and many complaints were the consequence. Almost all the Militia returned to town of their own accord, to the great indignation of the Governor, who issued some severe orders on such unmilitary-like behaviour. The fact was, the appearance of affairs looked so prosperous, that each day a flag of truce, with a confession of guilt and deprecation of punishment, was expected from the enemy; but the arrival of despatches from the camp at Chateaubelair, advertised the Colonists of an

Escape of the Caribs. event, no less surprising than extraordinary, that the Brigands had found means of avoiding the dangers which menaced them in the Carib country, by effecting a passage across the mountains, into their neighbourhood, where they had established a camp, and began to forage with impunity.

About this time, the evacuation of Saint Lucia by Brigadier General Stewart, opened an easy communication between that Island and Saint Vincent, the distance not exceeding six leagues. The enemy took the earliest

opportunity of sending across the channel a
Carib canoe, communicating an exact state-
ment of existing circumstances, and imploring
at the same time, an immediate reinforcement of men, with a supply of military and
other stores; the requisition was complied with
as expeditiously as possible, their affairs assumed a new appearance, and they took post
on a height at the extremity of Wallibo Estate, Their
where they were reconnoitered by the Thorn Camp at Wallibo.
Sloop of War, on the 2d of July, but she could
not bring her guns to bear upon them. The
same day the Roebuck also observed them,
and fired several shot from her forecastle and
quarter-deck guns, which apparently much
annoyed them; they were then supposed to Reinforce-
amount to about sixty persons, and were com- ment from St. Lucia.
posed of white and coloured French people.
They soon moved to Lafond's Hill, just above
Colonel Gordon's post at Chateaubelair, upon
which they began to fire, but without any
effect. In consequence, on the 6th, a party of
Regulars, and of the southern regiment of
Militia, and Rangers, the former under Lieutenant-Colonel Prevost, the latter under Major
Whytell, sailed to reinforce Colonel Gordon,

SECT. 5. but the calm weather prevented their arrival at Chateaubelair until the following day, and an attack was resolved on the next morning. The troops were divided in two parties, the one intended only to attract the attention of the enemy by a feint, the other marched at three o'clock in the morning, but from the difficulty Lafond's of access, did not gain the hill on which the Hill. enemy were posted, until daybreak, when they began a very spirited attack ; the enemy proved much more numerous than had been expected, and were supported by a two pound marmizette, which commanded a narrow pass, and injured the advancing party considerably, who finding they could not carry the place, were obliged to retreat. Lieutenant Moore of the forty-sixth, who led the storming party, being wounded, the troops halted for want of a leader; disorder soon pervaded the ranks, and a flight ensued, wherein a more than ordinary loss was sustained, twenty-three being killed, and forty-five wounded. Mr. William Greig and Thomas Grant, both Volunteers, were killed, the former gentleman was deeply regretted; Lieutenant Moore also died of his wounds. A flag of truce was sent requesting the body of Mr. Grant for interment, but the answer returned was that it had been already buried.

About this time, General Vaughan died at Martinico, and Major-General Paulus Æmilius Irving succeeded him in the command. In order to check the growing consequence of the Brigands in the Leeward Quarter, the Governor on the 12th July recalled Lieutenant-Colonel Leighton from Mount Young, with the forty-sixth regiment, and a detachment of Rangers, who arrived in town on the 14th, as Major Ecuyer could not spare any from Owia without endangering the post. These were embarked on the 16th with three six pound field pieces, and two howitzers, they landed at Troumaca, and marched to Bostock Park ; on the 18th our troops took possession of Fevrier's Ridge, without a shot being fired, which gave a complete command of the enemy's camp ; the next day a number of Negroes were observed going to the camp with provisions, followed by about ninety armed men ; these could have been severely handled, had the guns been placed in their positions ; before noon however, two guns and two mortars were got up, with ammunition, but they were not opened on the enemy, it being deemed necessary to wait for a third to place on another eminence ; previous to this, a part of the enemy from Morne Ronde, joined those at Lafond's Hill, notwithstanding detachments were stationed to prevent such communications. A party of about forty came as far down as they could, and fired on Colonel Gordon's post, but Lieutenant-Colonel Prevost gave orders not to return the fire, and got the mortar and guns loaded with grape, which he opened on them, and they immediately retired.

In consequence of the party on the Ridge having imprudently discovered themselves by firing one of the guns in order to ascertain the range, the enemy took the alarm, and silently effected their retreat in the night. In the morning their camp was taken possession of, where only some of their wounded were found. Intelligence was soon after received, that they Skirmishes were collected in the bed of the Morne a Garou at Morne a Garou, River, two parties were despatched after them, one of one hundred men, under Major Leith, to get into the bed of the river above the enemy, and another of the same force under Captain Douglas of the Engineers, to gain the river below them. The latter party could not get at them from the difficulty of their route, but they saw a party of about fifty, at a considerable distance. Major Leith's party however got upon the bank of the river, which they found so steep, that it was impossible to descend into it; but in searching for a passage, the enemy was discovered ascending the hill on the opposite side, in Indian files, towards Morne Cochon, within seventy yards distance; a fire was kept up on them, for upwards of two hours, while they were scrambling among the bushes to get up the hill, the troops being so advantageously posted, that the enemy could not bring a shot to bear upon them, until they were at least two hundred yards up. The Brigands formed as they got up, and commenced a fire upon the English from behind trees to cover their rear, as also a small field piece, which was at last observed carried by men on poles; they were repeatedly obliged to abandon it, and it could have been very easily taken, had it been possible to get across the ravine, but it was removed by them in the night, numbers must have been killed and

SECT. 5. wounded, as many were seen to drop in the bushes.

On the 22d the enemy were discovered in great force coming along the sea-side from their camp at Morne Ronde, directing their march up the dry ravine towards the pass into Rabacca. Major Leith with one hundred and fifty Rangers, was immediately dispatched from the post on Musement's Hill to dispute the passage with them, but arrived too late; the enemy had gained the top of the falls on the north side, whilst he was advancing on the south; however an engagement commenced as soon as the parties came opposite each other, across the ravine, and continued very warmly for three hours, until the ammunition of the English was expended, when it became necessary to retreat with thirteen wounded; a reinforcement of fifty Regulars, and a supply of ammunition was immediately sent, but the enemy did not await their return, a small party retiring beyond the falls towards Rabacca, and the remainder to their camp at Morne Ronde, which appears to have been their principal object. A mortar and two pieces of cannon

and at Musements.

were established on Musement's Hill, and for some days a few interchanges of artillery only took place. A Sloop and Schooner landed one hundred men, and ten women, on the night of the 23rd, from Guadaloupe, with a small mortar and marmizette; the Sloop Le Floreal was taken by the Thorn, and the Schooner chased into Saint Lucia. An attempt was made to take post on the opposite side of Morne Ronde, and troops were embarked from Musements for that purpose, but it was found impracticable.

On the 31st of July, a most diabolical outrage was committed by a party of about fifty, consisting of a few of the former French inhabitants, some free coloured persons, and negroes. They set fire to Mr. Gavin Hamilton's dwelling house, works, and negroe houses at Rose Hall, and killed about ten of his slaves, and wounded several; from thence they proceeded to Dr. Taits at Washilabo, where they burnt all the buildings, and inhumanly murdered Mr. Donald Munro, the manager. They were proceeding along the valley to Colonel Gordon's, but some negroes collected together, and Major Josias Jackson fortunately passing

SECT. 5. the bay in his canoe, with some of his slaves armed, landed and headed the party in pursuit of them, which these Brigands perceiving, they retreated precipitately without doing further damage. An attack on the camp at Morne Ronde having been concluded on, it was carried into execution on the morning of the 5th of August. The party ordered on that service marched at twelve o'clock on the night of the 4th, consisting of two hundred of the forty-sixth, and one hundred Rangers, the whole under the command of Captain Douglas of the Engineers. They took the road to the Souffriere, along the edge of which they proceeded, until they reached the ridge leading down to the enemy's camp; it was half past nine o'clock before the troops fell in with any of the enemy, when they were fired upon by the advanced picket in ambush, which after some resistance retired and joined the main body, who on the first alarm had marched out, and occupied a very advantageous position for opposing any advance, at a pass on a woody ridge, which effectually commanded their camp; a very obstinate engagement commenced here, which lasted upwards of an hour very disadvanta-

Attack at Morne Ronde.

geously for the English, as the situation did
not admit of a charge by the Regulars, but a
path was cut on each side of the ridge, by
which the Rangers got round, and as soon as
they made their appearance, the enemy gave
way, running off by the woods towards Duvallé's, abandoning their camp, with every
thing in it, without attempting any further resistance, although their numbers were superior
to those opposed to them; the Commandant
Massoteau, his Aide-de-Camp, and about twenty
others, were taken prisoners, some badly
wounded, but considerable numbers were got
off. Sixteen were found killed, the ammunition, field pieces, mortar, and a number of
small arms were taken. Their situation must
have been very distressing, as only a small
quantity of Cassada and salt was found in the
camp. The English troops were much dissatisfied on going out, having been badly
served with provisions for two days before, and
many of them wanted shoes, to which cause
their unusual backwardness may be ascribed.
Their loss was nine of the forty-sixth killed,
and thirty-three wounded, of the Rangers, three

killed and seven wounded; Dr. Oliver, an Ensign in the latter, died of his wounds.

The success in this affair fully compensated for recent disappointments, and promised greatly to facilitate the reduction of the enemy. Colonel Leighton deemed it advisable to maintain this newly acquired post, it being no doubt one of the strongest in the Island, and was the most advantageous of any to the enemy, from its favorable situation to receive their supplies from Saint Lucia; it was not deemed assailable any other way than the circuitous route by which the troops marched, and that had been rendered practicable by the enemy who had cutlassed the path up the Souffriere, which the troops followed : scouring parties were sent out to Duvallé's and Chatoyer's, where every thing was destroyed without opposition; several prisoners were taken, and many dead bodies found in the ravines. A party also went up Washilabo Valley to ascertain where the pass was, which was found to be in a northern direction, and came out above Rabacca. A post was established at Morne Ronde, and one at Richmond, and the troops were then withdrawn, and sent again to Mount Young, where they continued to destroy the provisions of the Caribs, and daily penetrated into the country; in one of these expeditions, Mr. William Grey, a Volunteer, with the Rangers fell into the hands of the enemy, and was doubtless immediately sacrificed; some parties also occasionally harassed the enemy from Owia, the aspect of affairs appeared exceedingly propitious and encouraging; when all at once a change was introduced, and a succession of misfortunes ensued.

On the 17th of August, Brigadier General Myers* arrived from Martinico, and succeeded to the command; from this gentleman great things were expected, but unfortunately for the Colony, these expectations were not realized. After the new Commander had obtained information of the existing state of affairs, and visited some of the most important posts committed to his care, he seemed resolved to make his first stroke, bold and decisive. He ordered Major Ecuyer, who commanded Owia, to move from that place, and to direct his march to- *General Myers arrived.*

* Lieutenant-General Sir William Myers, died at Barbados, August 1805.

SECT. 5. wards Mount Young, from whence he engaged to proceed with the main army towards Owia, consequently the enemy lying between, would be obliged to surrender at discretion, or be cut to pieces, the woods preventing their retreat on the one side, and the sea serving a similar purpose on the other, seemed to place success beyond the reach of doubt. Conformably to his instructions, Major Ecuyer took the field, and obliged the enemy to retire, as he advanced; having gone as far as he thought he might, without exposing himself to be cut off, he waited three or four days in the open air, under arms, for the promised junction of the General; at length vexed with disappointment, and his troops exhausted with fatigue, he returned again to Owia, and dispatched Captain Law, of the forty-sixth, to head quarters, to notify what had been done, and to receive further orders. The whole force however remained inactive for some days, which allowed the enemy to collect their parties, and on the night of the 3rd of September, they made an attack on the post at Owia, in three columns, one of which succeeded in attracting the attention of the troops, while the other two rushed in from the opposite

Owia taken.

side; the contest lasted some time, and the enemy are said to have suffered greatly. But the darkness of the night created great confusion on both sides, and two of the enemy's columns are said to have fired on each other for some time, the same error was also ascribed to the English troops; Major Ecuyer who commanded, notwithstanding he had received two wounds, was enabled by assistance, to get away some distance, but was unfortunately overtaken next morning, and murdered. All the officers were missing, but in a day or two, three came in, and Dr. Baillie was taken prisoner, and sent to Guadaloupe, from whence he returned some time in December following,* so that the loss was reduced to four officers killed, and thirty-one men; those who escaped were taken off the rocks by the boats of his Majesty's ship Experiment, Captain Barrett,† who distin-

---

* Dr. Baillie related that the day after the surprise, the commanding officer, Marinier, directed the English party to bury their dead, in doing which, they were fired upon by the enemy, and one man was killed; this so enraged Marinier, that he rushed out among his own people, cut one down, wounded another, and put an officer in confinement.

† Captain Barrett, R. N. was lost in the Minotaur seventy-four, at the mouth of the Texel, on the 22d December 1810.

SECT. 5. guished himself by his humane exertions, as likewise did Mr. Frith of the Fanny : some of the men effected their escape through the woods to Morne Ronde.

The loss of this post proved the loss of many ; the very moment the enemy conceived themselves in the tenable possession of it, they dispatched a canoe with the intelligence to Saint Lucia, and solicited strongly a reinforcement, which was honoured with the most ready compliance. On the 15th of September, four vessels from thence anchored at Owia, and landed about five hundred men with provisions and stores. The English cruisers having fallen to leeward during the calm weather which prevailed, could not come up with them. In consequence of this intelligence, it was deemed expedient by the Commander-in-Chief, to evacuate Mount Young, and orders to this effect were transmitted to Lieutenant-Colonel Leighton, who commanded there. About nine o'clock on the night of the 19th, the troops marched away with the artillery, leaving their huts illuminated. The next evening they reached Biabou, where a party of Caribs made their appearance, these were spies upon their retreat, and waited to avail themselves of any opportunity that might offer to harass the rear : having brought forward the troops stationed there, the detachment reached Sion Hill on the 21st, and were distributed among the several posts encircling the town. General Myers thought it necessary to maintain the occupancy of the Vigie, but having omitted to supply it with provisions and other stores, the garrison had only the means of subsisting parsimoniously for three days. On the evening of the 22nd, the enemy appeared in great numbers at Mariaqua Valley, and early on the following morning, were found posted on Fairbairn's Ridge, having completely cut off the communication between the Vigie and the town, and drove off the cattle from the Fountain and Belair Estates.

The safety of the Vigie became now the object of the general concern, its situation being such as would not admit of delay, eighty mules were loaded with supplies, and set forward under the command of Lieutenant-Colonel Ritchie, with a party of about three hundred Regulars and Rangers ; they kept the high road until they arrived at Calliaqua, and then

SECT. 5. continued their route through Pradies and
Harmony Hall, and Raguet's negroe-grounds,
until they fell into Belmont road at the extremity of Fairhall, when they were fired upon
by the enemy, and an action commenced which
was of a short duration. When the troops
gained the summit of the ridge, and obliged
the enemy to abandon a Galba Fence which
they occupied, and fall back, Captain Foster of
the forty-sixth, who commanded in front, perceiving their declining state, gave orders for
an immediate charge, but not an individual
would obey him.* The troops most disgrace-
fully gave way just in the moment of victory,
and fled in different directions, closely pursued
by the enemy. The greatest part of the provisions fell into their hands, and the loss was
estimated at about sixty killed and taken
prisoners; in all probability the whole detachment would have been cut off, had they
not found shelter beneath the guns of Fort

* It seems the troops were dissatisfied with the stoppage
of a part of their allowances, and the officers of the Rangers
were involved in disputes with the committee respecting
their pay, so that they paid no attention to the discipline of
their men, and consequently this disaster occurred.

Duvernette, which were assiduously plied by Major Henry Sharpe; Colonel Ritchie, being entirely cut off in his retreat, collected as many officers and men as he could together, amounting in the whole to about thirty, and retreated to the Prospect Estate, and threw himself into the mill there, and behind the ruins of the buildings, where he defended himself for several hours against a large body of the enemy, who made several unsuccessful attempts to force him, in which they lost many men, and about dark, finding all their efforts vain, they retired. At midnight, the small party abandoned the mill, and marched to the Villa Estate works, where they remained for the night, and next morning took refuge in Fort Duvernette. It is remarkable that not one of these men throughout this long sustained assault, received the slightest hurt, except their gallant commander, who was wounded in the leg by a musket shot on stepping out of the mill to reconnoitre, of which he died shortly after; he was much beloved and died regretted. Michael Keane of the Rangers was the only officer killed in the previous action.

The consternation and dread occasioned by the above unhappy defeat, were excessive, an immediate attack on the outposts was apprehended, which were considerably weakened by the absence of the detachment, now given over for lost, besides as an additional circumstance of distress, the situation of the troops in the Vigie was desperate; the want of provisions laid it under the unavoidable necessity of surrendering at discretion, however improbable the expectation of mercy might be in so doing. Nothing however was neglected that could add to the security of the island. The fortunate escape of so many of Lieutenant-Colonel Ritchie's party, which arrived in Kingstown on the 25th, rendered the situation of the town less precarious; the old French post on Kelly's Ridge was taken possession of, and put in a very defensible state. Orders were sent to Captain Molesworth who commanded at Morne Ronde, for the evacuation of that post, and two negroe messengers were procured to carry letters by different routes to the Vigie, to the same effect, one of whom named Thomas Nash, a Ranger, succeeded in getting in on the morn-

ing of the 26th, with great dexterity, he was
rewarded with twenty Johannes and his freedom; the other returned.

The same afternoon Brigadier General Myers
marched from Dorsetshire Hill with a large
detachment, and took post on Baker's Estate,
now called Cane Hall, opposite to the enemy
on Fairbairn's Ridge, where he remained until
dark, and then returned. This feint succeeded
in having the desired effect, the enemy were
induced to draw off their other posts about the
Vigie, and concentrate their whole force on this
side. Captain Cope of the sixtieth regiment,
who commanded at the Vigie, according to the
orders which so fortunately reached him, evacuated it at the early hour of seven, taking the
advantage of a heavy shower that fell about
that time; he went down by the Carapan
Estate, where he fell into the high road, along
which he continued his march unperceived by
the enemy, until he arrived at Calliaqua, where
boats were waiting to receive and convey them
to Sir William Young's Island, and the Rock,
from whence they were brought down to Kingstown next morning; the acquisition of these
men, together with those under Captain Moles-

sect. 5. worth from Morne Ronde, who arrived in the night of the 27th, contributed greatly towards the strengthening of such posts as were conceived to be immediately in danger, and recalled hope to the inhabitants. The Vigie becoming once more the possession of the enemy, the town was continually harassed with the fear of an attack, and therefore to avoid the effects of a surprise, the greatest vigilance was observed, and the extremes of duty submitted to by every individual; indeed the danger appeared so near, and so considerable, that it was impossible for the principle of self preservation to slumber in any breast.

SECTION VI.

Arrival of the fortieth, fifty-fourth, and fifty-ninth regiments with General Irving—Attack of the Vigie—Evacuation by the Enemy—March to Colonarie—General Stewart—English Camp taken—Arrival of General Hunter—The Troops withdrawn to Kingstown—The Vigie occupied by the Enemy—Skirmishes at Miller's Ridge.

THUS were the unfortunate inhabitants continued the prey of anxiety, and the subjects of fatigue until the evening of the 29th of September, when His Majesty's ship Scipio, and several Transports appeared in sight to leeward ; as calm weather prevailed, Captain Barrett ordered all the small vessels in the bay to go down to the fleet, for the purpose of taking out the troops, and several hundred landed that night. The next day the Transports came into the bay, when part of the fortieth regiment commanded by Major Harcourt, the fifty-fourth by Lieutenant-Colonel Godday Strutt,* and the fifty-ninth by Lieutenant-Colonel Francis

* Major-General Strutt, now Governor of Quebec, 1829.

sect. 6. Fuller,* were landed. These regiments had only returned a few weeks from the continent before embarkation; Major-General Irving† also arrived, having been appointed by the Commander-in-Chief, General Leigh, to this command. Nothing passed in town of which the enemy were not apprised; they retired from their position on Fairbairn's Ridge, and made every possible provision to maintain the occupancy of the Vigie. The necessary preparations being made, Lieutenant-Colonel Strutt, and Lieutenant-Colonel Leith of the Rangers, with a detachment of seven hundred and fifty men, marched on the night of the 1st of October, about ten o'clock, round by Calliaqua, and proceeded to the heights of Calder Estate, the

Attack on the Vigie. east side of the Vigie, and gained their situation about three in the morning. ˉ Generals Irving and Myers, with the principal body, consisting of the Artillery under Major Duvernette, the fifty-ninth under Lieutenant-Colonel Fuller, the flank companies of the fifty-fourth, four companies of the fortieth, and the remains

* Francis Fuller, a General of 1825.

† Sir Paulus Æmilius Irving, Bart. a General of 1812, died 1828.

of the forty-sixth, under Lieutenant-Colonel Leighton, the whole amounting to about nine hundred men, marched from Sion Hill and Arno's Vale about two o'clock, proceeding up Warrawarou Valley. On crossing the river, Lieutenant-Colonel Leighton with a part of the forty-sixth, and two guns were detached to go round by Calliaqua, and at the Fountain Estate pasture, the flank companies of the fifty-fourth and fifty-ninth, with the four companies of the fortieth, under Captain Boland* of the latter, were also detached up the valley, with orders to gain the heights by Debuques; the fifty-ninth struck off to the right at the pasture, and gained Fairbairn's Ridge, from which they drove off one of the enemy's pickets; the artillery having joined the fifty-ninth on the Ridge, the whole halted about half way from the top, which Major M'Leod with that regiment was ordered to gain.

During this time, the detachment that had been ordered to proceed by Debuque's had been attacked by the enemy in their ascent to the

---

* John Boland, Lieutenant-Colonel, 1812; his brother also was present a Captain in the same regiment, and died a Lieutenant-Colonel.

SECT. 6. place where the house formerly stood, to gain which, they had to cross a deep rivulet, and then ascend a steep hill covered with brushwood; the enemy advantageously posted behind trees and bushes, galled the advancing troops much, and before they were able to drive them off, they had the misfortune to sustain a con-

Evacuation siderable loss of officers and men ;* the enemy
by the
Enemy. however fled precipitately on the troops approaching, and the possession of the Mariaqua, or Vigie Ridge, was obtained without further opposition ; the fifty-ninth had the same object in view, but they were opposed by the enemy from a thick wood about the summit, who had also thrown up a small work ; from the advantage of the enemy's position, and the steepness of the ground, rendered more difficult from the heavy rains, it would appear to have been

* " The Grenadiers of the fifty-ninth, were advanced in a wood on the side of a steep hill, where to their great surprise, they suffered very considerable loss, as the enemy was a long distance from them ; at length it was discovered that the fire came from the tops of the trees, immediately above them, a party of Caribs having concealed themselves among the branches. A volley fired at the tops of the trees brought down seven men, the rest soon followed." Stewart's Sketches, Vol. I. p. 136, note.

deemed impracticable to force them : the firing
which began about seven o'clock, continued
furiously the whole day between the two parties,
at only about fifty yards distance, without any
ground being gained or lost on either side,
although the enemy made three attempts to
charge.   A brisk fire was also kept up at times
from the artillery; the principal force of the
enemy was early in the day brought to this
point, and not more than fifty men were left
on the Vigie, when Lieutenant-Colonel Leith
proposed that the place should be stormed, but
the General would not consent to make such
an operation which must have proved decisive.
In the afternoon the remaining four companies
of the fortieth, which had been left at Dorsetshire Hill, joined the Generals on Fairbairn's
Ridge, and with part of the forty-sixth, were
stationed with the artillery.   Lieutenant-Colonel Strutt's party at Calder Ridge, endeavoured
to conceal themselves in the canes, waiting for
further orders, but a party of Caribs that
passed along the road near them, being fired
at and some killed, they were discovered from
the Vigie, and some shot fired at them from a
four pounder, but without effect; the front of

SECT. 6. the party was advanced within musket-shot under the Vigie; about two hundred Caribs took post at Aker's Hill, but just as Lieutenant-Colonel Strutt had resolved to charge them, they retired. About three o'clock he received orders to retreat, and the party joined the Generals at Fairbain's Ridge. The detachment under Captain Boland, after gaining the Ridge, advanced within musket-shot of the enemy, when they halted for orders, which were sent them to retreat; the guns that were sent round by Calliaqua, with the forty-sixth, could not proceed from the deepness of the roads, and were obliged to return that night to Sion Hill. Towards night, the fire between the fifty-ninth and the enemy, was remarkably heavy, but slackened as darkness came on; about seven o'clock, the troops were withdrawn, and orders given to retreat; it is supposed that the enemy had the advantage in that respect, and retired previously; one of the English guns fell over the ridge, and was obliged to be left behind. The troops behaved remarkably well, but experienced a loss of upwards of one hundred killed or wounded, principally the latter; this was the more severely regretted, as the object aimed at was not obtained. The SECT. 6. enemy seeing themselves surrounded by so numerous a body of brave and determined men, could expect nothing less than an immediate attack on the Vigie, the consequence of which must have been, that they would have been all cut off; they therefore took the advantage of the darkness of the early part of the night to make their escape, for a retreat it could not be called; but, the extraordinary part of this day's proceedings is, that the English retreated also at the same time, the reasons for so doing, could only be apparent to the two Generals, as their conduct appeared unaccountable to the rest of the army; it is still more extraordinary that General Irving should have obtained the thanks of the Commander-in-Chief, and the Colonial Secretary, for his capture of the Vigie.

A non-commissioned officer, and about ten men, missed their road on the retreat, and in wandering up and down, fell in with a negro who undertook to conduct them to town, but led them towards the Vigie, with an intention of delivering them up to the enemy; on perceiving that they had fled, he followed them,

SECT. 6. and the serjeant took possession of the post, where he remained until the next morning, when an account of the evacuation reached General Irving, who ordered out a party of Rangers under Lieutenant Kelly, to take possession of it; but an eccentric character, James Kirkwood, who had joined the serjeant and his party, considered his possession of the post as paramount, and refused to deliver it without a receipt being signed for it, which was acceded to, and the British flag displayed.

For several days after the unfortunate 2nd of October, unsteadiness and inactivity seemed to pervade every measure; the fifty-fourth regiment was at one time embarked for Grenada, and after remaining on board some days, was relanded, and on the 10th, marched out to Stubbs'. About the same time the forty-sixth regiment, and General Myers' Rangers also marched to windward, the fifty-ninth with the Island Rangers had before taken post, first at Akers' Hill, and afterwards at Jambou Works. But during this disgraceful imbecility, the enemy had time to dispatch a canoe to Saint Lucia, and obtain a supply of ammunition and other necessaries, which determined

March to Colonarie.

them to intrench themselves on Moung Young
and Mount William, and wait any advance
that might be made. They were first discovered at the former post by Captain Pack-
wood of the Army brig. About the 16th,
the army sat down opposite those positions on
Bellevue Ridge. On the 18th, General Irving
with a part of the army, crossed the Colonarie
River, and took possession of the north ridge
of the Colonarie Vale, when two well directed
shot were fired at the troops by the enemy
from two small field pieces upon Mount William, which having passed very near the General, the troops were instantly ordered to retreat to Bellevue. This unexpected salutation
confirmed the idea that the enemy had been
employed in getting artillery on the works of
Mount William; soon after a movement was
made, and batteries were erected on the ridges
opposite to Mount William, which fired shot
and shells with little intermission, but without
much effect, as the enemy sheltered themselves
behind the ridge; some skirmishes, the natural
consequence of the proximity of two hostile
armies, took place with little loss on either side
until the 30th of October, when Colonel Gra-

ham with a party was ordered to gain a ridge called Blackett's Bluff,* the peculiar advantage of which the enemy readily perceived, and drew from that post almost all their force to oppose him, which the General observing, ordered Colonel Graham to retreat, which was done before he could obtain his object, and in the retreat four men were killed, and sixteen wounded, principally Rangers; Adjutant Brown of that corps, died of his wounds.

Thus the fairest opportunity that could have presented itself of cutting off the enemy after they had gone out of Mount William to oppose Colonel Graham's party, was that day lost, and also of taking possession of that important post. Several slaves who came in from the enemy, represented their situation in the most distressing light, they were driven to subsist on the mules they had with them, which were nearly expended; the enemy, exclusive of the Caribs, were not more than three hundred; it was said in justification of this inactivity of the

---

* Blackett's Bluff is a ridge on the north of Colonarie Pasture, it is so named from a Captain in the thirty-first regiment, who first established a post there in 1772, after the British troops had landed at Grand Sable.

British Commander, that he was in possession of orders not to act offensively, but to wait for the reinforcement on its passage. These orders must have been framed in entire ignorance of the strength and situation of the enemy. The public opinion was strongly expressed in a re- solution entered into by the inhabitants on the 22d of October, when it was resolved, that an address be presented to Major-General Leigh, Commander-in-Chief of His Majesty's troops in the Windward Islands, thanking him for his great attention to the interests of the Colony, in sending over so respectable a force, as the three gallant regiments lately arrived from England, and that Henry Haffey, and Joseph Warner, Esquires, be requested to present the same, and also to represent to General Leigh the inactive situation in which the army in this Island is at present, and all other matters that shall be transmitted to them.

General Stewart arrived on the 17th October from Martinico, and relieved General Myers. And on the 30th November, General Irving re- turned to Martinico; on his resignation, the command devolved upon Brigadier General Stewart, he uniformly adopted a similar system

SECT. 6. of conduct with his predecessor, which in the end produced his own defeat, and well nigh effected the ruin of the Colony. On the 8th of December, a party of the enemy took possession of the same hill as on a former occasion, and when the morning gun was fired, they returned a volley of musketry upon the artillery and Grenadiers of the fifty-fourth regiment; the compliment was immediately returned, and after an hours firing, the enemy retired; they appeared to be about fifty in number without a white man among them, and had thrown up a slight entrenchment during the night.

A flying corps of negroes was subscribed for by the proprietors in Mariaqua, Biabou, and Jambou, for the purpose of ranging those heights and woods, and were put under the command of Mr. Duprey and Mr. Laborde. About the 15th, the former surprised a small party at Greig's Ridge, and took them prisoners, and continued to harass the foraging parties of the enemy, who were obliged to send for plantains to the heights of Massarica, where there were abundance. On the 17th, one hundred and fifty of the enemy attacked the covering party at the ridge on the Union Estate; this post consisted only of eighteen men, Regulars and Rangers, who were joined by six negroes belonging to the estate at the commencement of the attack; such however was the gallant behaviour of this small party, that they kept the enemy at bay for upwards of half an hour, under a very severe fire, when they were joined by a small picket of the fifty-ninth regiment, and a reinforcement of about thirty men of the same regiment appearing in sight at the same time, the enemy retreated leaving three dead, one an officer; from the traces of blood on the road the enemy went off by, their wounded must have been considerable; the English loss was one Ranger killed, and one Regular wounded.

On the morning of the 8th of January, 1796, a more tragical catastrophe happened than any which had yet been experienced. General Stewart had injudiciously weakened the main position he occupied by multiplying from time to time an unnecessary number of picket guards; this circumstance, with others, were communicated to the Brigands by two soldiers, who having robbed the provision store, and dreading the punishment, deserted to the enemy.   The attack commenced on the left of the encampment, about four o'clock, just after firing the morning gun.   Somewhat advanced up the ridge on that side was a small battery of one field piece, and a cohorn, which that night was under the charge of Lieutenant Panton of the fifty-ninth, with about twenty men.   Mons. Chenou, a Frenchman from Saint Lucia, succeeded in surprising two of the sentries posted a good way in advance of this battery, both of whom were stabbed by him; he also advanced and shot a third in front of the work, then leaped through the embrasure, when he was immediately seized and made prisoner by a serjeant of the fifty-ninth, who was about to put him to death, but was prevented by Lieutenant Verity of the fifty-fourth. The enemy were led thus far by one of the deserters, who then left them and returned. Lieutenant Panton with his party, was soon obliged to relinquish the battery, from the numbers and impetuosity with which the enemy rushed in upon him; he fell back on the fifty-fourth, and one discharge of grape was fired at him in his retreat, but which did no mischief.   After this success, the enemy lost

English Camp taken.

no time in pursuing their advantage, the gun having the command of the entire ridge occupied by the artillery, the whole in a short time was entirely lost; they pushed on immediately, obtained possession of the other batteries, and obliged the troops to abandon their ground, and retreat to Bellevue Ridge, on which they were covered by Major M'Leod, who with part of the fifty-ninth, was posted there; twelve pieces of brass ordnance were left in the camp which the enemy took possession of, and then attempted to cut off the English in their retreat from Bellevue, by occupying the different ridges commanding the high road. This, according to existing appearances, they could have effected with very little difficulty, having every advantage on their side. Fortunately however Lieutenant-Colonel Fuller, who with a party of about two hundred men, had marched from Biabou that morning in their way out to the camp, fell in with and soon routed them. After halting some time at Bellevue, and sending forward the wounded, the troops continued their retreat towards Kingstown, in which they were much harassed by the enemy; that night they halted at Biabou, and next day took position

SECT. 6. on Aker's Hill, Calder Heights, and other places in that neighbourhood. The loss was great, especially in officers wounded, who all exerted themselves by every means in their power to prevent the disaster which befel them; Volunteers Simmons and Ashburner were killed, sixteen officers wounded, and one prisoner, and one hundred and thirty-five privates either killed or wounded.*

To judge from the picture of the past, nothing was expected from General Stewart, that could promise a reverse of circumstances, although he exhibited most consummate personal gallantry; the community looking back on the series of misfortunes he had encountered, gave up all for lost, and seemed sinking beneath the apprehension. This arose in the general opinion from the dilatory, weak, and unsteady measures of General Irving, and his pertinacity in declining to consult with, and refusing all advice, not only from his officers, but from the inhabitants of the Colony, who had firmly, with much less considerable forces, not only defended themselves, but acted offensively against

* Bryan Edwards states the loss at four hundred. Vol. IV. p. 67.

the enemy with success. No doubt was enter- tained that the reinforcement under this General was fully adequate to the purposes of reducing the opposing enemy, under the conduct of an active and spirited officer.

In this anxious and desponding hour, Major Arrival of General Hunter arrived from Martinico on the General Hunter. 12th of January, and as the highest opinion was entertained of his abilities, a proportionate confidence was reposed in him ; immediately on his landing, he made himself acquainted with the position and state of the army; his resolutions were instantaneous ; except the strong post of the Vigie, he drew the whole force into the heights about the town, and The troops withdrawn having strengthened all the passes, secured the to Kingstown. sovereignty of the Island against any attempts the enemy might have the temerity to make.

On the morning of the 14th, the enemy appeared in great numbers in Mariaqua Valley, and seemed determined to attack the Vigie with all their force ; but General Hunter, aware of the design, and a combination of circumstances rendering the place at this time unimportant, gave orders for its evacuation, and the The Vigie occupied by enemy instantly marched in. This possession the Enemy.

SECT. 6. so flattering to their views, was succeeded the ensuing day by an advance on Baker's Ridge, where they brought up a small field piece and mortar, and fixed a picket guard close under the redoubt on Miller's Ridge; on the night of the 18th they began to fire shot and shells, but so injudiciously, that they did no execution whatever. At the same time a considerable party of Caribs crossed over the hill above Miller's Ridge, and encamped themselves about Bow Wood, at the head of Kingstown Valley. At day light, on the morning of the 20th, an attack was made upon the enemy at Baker's Ridge, from Miller's redoubt by Lieutenant-Colonel Prevost of the sixtieth: the ground between this post and the enemy was excessively steep, rugged, and broken, and covered with a thick wood, and the ridge down which Lieutenant-Colonel Prevost descended, was in many places so narrow, that two men could scarcely march abreast; near the bottom at the extremity of the wood, on a small flat, the enemy had a large party very strongly posted; the object intended was to dislodge them; but from these impediments, together with the misfortune of Lieutenant-Colonel Prevost being severely wounded in two places, early in the attack, the attempt did not succeed. The troops returned to the ridge with the loss of a few men, having surprised and cut to pieces the advanced picket guard.

This affair however led to one of much more consequence, the enemy followed closely in the retreat, and actually advanced within a few yards of the ridge, where Major M'Leod of the fifty-ninth was stationed, which brought on an action that continued the whole day; the enemy making repeated attempts to gain the ridge in different parts, and being as repeatedly repulsed with great loss, the Militia were again inspired with confidence from a Volunteer party distinguishing themselves considerably in this affair, Alexander Cruikshank, Alexander Cumming, George Burgess, John Dallaway, and James Campbell, being at the head of it; Major Josias Jackson with a party of Island Rangers, also attacked the Caribs, who had crossed over to Green Hill, and taken possession of Bow Wood House; after a considerable firing, they were routed with the loss of several killed, and in their retreat they set fire to the house, into which they threw such of their

SECT. 6. dead as were within their reach. Soon after this attack commenced, Major Fraser came up with a reinforcement, and the quarter was effectually cleared of the enemy; the English loss was estimated at fifty killed and wounded.

In the height of the action on this day, the ship Brunswick arrived with three hundred men of the sixty-third, under the command of Lieutenant-Colonel Gower; this was a third time that the opportune arrival of succours, when dismay and danger predominated in all ranks, again raised the Colonists from despondency; indeed as soon as the first panic had subsided, the most vigorous measures were adopted by the inhabitants for their defence; the Committee of expenditure and defence offered bounties and encouragements to such Volunteers as would enlist; Lieutenant-Colonel Haffey was indefatigable in his exertions. Lieutenant-Colonel Leith, Major Fraser, Captains Alves and Ross, and other officers of the Rangers, soon formed a body of three hundred Volunteers; Major Josias Jackson also raised another corps. Lieutenant-Colonel Fairbairn with some of the principal inhabitants, mustered to act as Dragoons: the small remains of the southern regiment of Militia joined the different corps with alacrity; every heart and hand seemed devoted to second the able General, who had been sent to save the Island from destruction, and its proprietors from ruin.

On the 21st, Major M'Leod, who commanded at Miller's Redoubt, surprised a picket of the enemy advanced within thirty yards of his post in a thick wood; they fled so precipitately as to leave a number of muskets, cartouch boxes, and other articles behind them; the Major, although much disabled from former exertions, supported himself with the greatest calmness and resolution. Captain Edward French of the Militia, with a small party of the fifty-ninth, made a spirited attack on the enemy and routed them, but was himself badly wounded; after this the enemy began to retire from their position at Bakers', contenting themselves with firing shot and shells at Dorsetshire Hill and Miller's Redoubt, several shot fired at the former came over the hill and lodged in town, and one fell into the bay, but without mischief. On the 23rd and following day, they made a shew of intrenching themselves, but on a six pound field piece being got up to Miller's

Ridge, and immediately opened on their encampment, evident confusion was clearly discerned among them; that night they suddenly moved off with their artillery, and commenced fortifying themselves in and about the Vigie; considerable numbers of dead bodies were found in and near their encampment. By accounts of negroes who deserted from them, they lost one of their principal officers, and another had been shot by themselves; their wounded were removed to Grand Sable, and a fresh company sent in their place; of the artillery taken at Colonarie, they only brought forward one field piece and a mortar. On the 7th of April, four men of the sixtieth deserted to the enemy, when one named Bradshaw was promoted by Marinier to a company, and on the 8th was intrusted with the command of two hundred men to surprise the picket at Arno's Vale, but failed in the attempt; he was wounded and taken prisoner, and hanged the following day.

SECTION VII.

*Arrival of General Abercromby—Attack on the Vigie
—Surrender of the French—General Orders—
Caribs retreat—Their Removal to Balliceaux—
Exertions of the Rangers, and general Surrender
—Removal to Rattan—Expences of the War.*

A PAUSE took place in the operations on both
sides for some time. General Abercromby
arrived at Barbados on the 17th of March with
his army, and on the 22d, embarked on an expedition against Saint Lucia, where the troops
were landed on the 27th, and the principal
forts were attacked and taken, on which the
Island was surrendered on condition of the
white and free coloured persons being sent to
England as prisoners of war.* This was disastrous intelligence for the Brigands of Saint
Vincent; their principal resource for reinforcements and supplies were cut off, and a deserter
from the Vigie gave information that they had

* Among the deserters taken and executed was Collins,
the man who led the enemy into the English camp at Colonarie.

been made acquainted with their misfortune, and their discontent at their situation had much increased in consequence.

After this conquest, General Abercromby arrived at Saint Vincent on the 3d of June, and in the course of the following day, all the fleet with the troops came into the bay. The Governor, addressed a letter to the inhabitants congratulating them on the circumstance, and requesting, " on the troops moving to windward, every loyal subject would join Lieutenant-Colonel Hartley at Sion Hill, who would there make such a distribution as might be necessary, for the preservation of the Town of Kingstown." The General's presence having been required at Carriacou, an Island within the Government of Grenada, he returned from thence on the 7th, and the troops having been landed, and cantoned on Sion Hill, Cane Garden and Arno's Vale Estates, on the afternoon of the 9th, they marched in the following order :

First column commanded by Brigadier General Knox.

200 Lowensteins Riflemen,
100 Haffey's Rangers,   } to Mariaqua Valley.
636 of the 14th regiment,

Second, commanded by Major-General Hunter.

50	Lowenstein's Riflemen,	
100	Haffey's Rangers,	to Calder Ridge with a
314	42nd regiment,	a brass twelve pounder,
531	53rd regiment,	and 5½ inch mortar.
50	Pioneers,	

Third, commanded by Major General Morshead.

50	Lowenstein's Riflemen,	
50	Jackson's Rangers,	to Carapan Ridge with a
254	Buffs,	brass twelve pounder,
450	York Rangers,	and a 5½ inch mortar.
50	Pioneers,	

Fourth, commanded by Lieutenant-Colonel Fuller.

40	Jackson's Rangers,	to Belmont Ridge with
220	of 59th Regiment,	two long brass six
263	63rd regiment,	pounders.
50	Pioneers,	

Fifth, commanded by Lieutenant-Colonel Dickens.

260	2nd West India regiment,*	up Warrawarou Valley.
57	34th regiment,	

Sixth, (Reserve) under Lieutenant-Colonel Spencer.†

145	40th regiment,	to follow the line of
87	54th regiment,	march;

making a total of three thousand nine hundred

* Lewis Grant, a Major General 1819, and Governor of Trinidad 1829, served as a Lieutenant in this regiment.

† Sir Brent Spencer, G. C. B. a General 1825, distinguished himself in the Peninsular war, and died 1829.

SECT. 7. and sixty men. The columns gained their several positions that night or early next morning without any material occurrence, except the falling in with three of the enemy at Stubbs', two of whom were killed, and the accident of part of Lieutenant-Colonel Dickens' division separating from the main body in the darkness of the night; the Lieutenant-Colonel however gained possession of the right of the enemy's position at Louis Patiences before day light, an important pass, from which the enemy, principally Caribs, fled without making much resistance, and where he planted the colours of the thirty-fourth regiment. Lieutenant-Colonel Dickens attempted to carry a strong and commanding post a little to the left of the former, but did not succeed, and suffered materially in the attack; the Caribs from the woods, and the enemy at the post kept up a smart fire, both with shot and shells, and at last got up a swivel which was only fired twice, without any effect; he maintained his ground however but with the loss of three officers, and fifty-one men killed or wounded.

Attack on the Vigie. The columns under Generals Hunter and Morshead, began to cannonade the old Vigie

from Calder and Carapan Ridges, between six
and seven o'clock in the morning, the former
distant about five hundred yards, the latter
three hundred, while an unremitting discharge
of musketry was kept up by the men from the
adjoining canes, and other situations near the
enemy's works. The column under Lieutenant-
Colonel Fuller, was delayed considerably by
the difficulties they encountered in getting on
their artillery, however they soon overcame
them, and opened their fire in front of the
foundation of the old house at Belmont. In a
short time the effects of this fire were visibly
great on the old Vigie, and orders were in consequence issued to storm it, which were executed
about two o'clock, with a promptitude and
celerity that reflected honour on the troops;
with Colonel Blair of the Buffs, and Major
Stewart of the 42d, they instantly carried the
post, the enemy retreating with great precipitation to their other works; this success was
followed up with unabating ardour and intrepidity, and the two succeeding works fell into
the possession of the English. The impetuosity of the troops was such, that Lieutenant
David Stewart with about thirty men rushed

SECT. 7. on to the New Vigie, and had actually got within a few yards of it when they were recalled.

After this, a cessation of firing took place on both sides until about five o'clock, when the artillery was about to open, and the troops prepared to storm this their dernier resort; a flag of truce was sent out to General Abercromby with an offer of submission, which was accepted on the terms of delivering up the other posts of Owia, Rabacca, and Mount Young, with their garrisons; but the officer who came with the flag, importuning the General to include the French inhabitants, and the Island negroes who were in arms with them; and the General wishing to consult the Governor on the subject, the business was not Surrender finally concluded until nine o'clock the next of the French. morning, and at noon they marched out with the honours of war, laid down their arms, to the number of four hundred and sixty men, and were conducted to Kingstown, and immediately embarked on board the vessels in the harbour. The English loss amounted to about forty killed, and one hundred and forty-one wounded; the loss of the enemy was estimated at not more than half that number. Marinier SECT. 7. with his principal officers, were embarked on board the Experiment, amid the execrations of the spectators. Captain Douglas of the Engineers died of his wounds much regretted; Volunteer Gordon, Captain M'Lean, and Lieutenant Houston were killed.

The general orders issued on the occasion were as follow: " The Commander-in-Chief has the greatest satisfaction in publicly acknowledging that the success of His Majesty's arms on the 10th, proceeded from the information he had received from Major General Hunter, and from the local knowledge of the ground, communicated to him by the gentlemen of the Colony, who not only pointed out the route by which the columns marched, but likewise conducted them; the plan was carried into full execution by the good conduct of the officers, and the intrepidity of the men. Lieutenant-General Abercromby begs leave to return his best thanks to Major Generals Hunter and Morshead, Brigadier General Knox, Lieutenant-Colonels Fuller and Dickens who conducted the different columns. Lieutenant-Colonel Dickens and the troops who served

SECT. 7. under him, are entitled to a great share of praise, and the Commander-in-Chief is much obliged to Brigadier General Knox, for the well timed reinforcement which he sent them. The Buffs and Royal Highlanders who carried the first work, the fifty-ninth and sixty-third regiments, the York Rangers, and the detachment of Lowensteins, who had all an opportunity of distinguishing themselves, deserve the Commander-in-Chief's warmest approbation; he regrets the temporary loss which the service sustains from the wound which Captain Douglas of the Royal Engineers received during the attack, his knowledge of the Island, and his professional abilities, make the loss of his assistance at this time to be particularly felt. Sir Ralph Abercromby observed with peculiar satisfaction the great skill with which the Royal Artillery was conducted under Major Smith. Another opportunity presented itself of acknowledging the services rendered by the Royal Navy from the assistances granted by Captain Wolley,* and in the exertions of the seamen under Captain Barrett. The General would fail in his duty if he did not express his fullest

* Thomas Wolley, Vice Admiral of the White, died 1826.

approbation of the good conduct, intelligence, and courage of the Island Rangers, under the command of Lieutenant-Colonel Haffey, and Major Josias Jackson. Sir Ralph Abercromby begs leave to return his thanks to Lieutenant-Colonel Fairbairn for his attention to him, and services on the 10th instant, as well as upon all occasions."

Lieutenant - Colonel Spencer, with about seven hundred men, marched out to the Windward Quarter, and took possession of Mount William and Mount Young on the 14th; Lieutenant-Colonel James Stewart, with the forty-second, took post at Colonarie, and Lieutenant Colonel Graham at Rabacca; the enemy had buried the remainder of the guns they had taken in the unfortunate affair at Colonarie, and it was not until after some threats were made, that they discovered where they were concealed. The sixty-third regiment under Lieutenant-Colonel Gower, who were sent round in His Majesty's ship Ulysses, to take possession of Owia, were prevented by the boisterous weather from landing, and obliged to return. The French officer at the post however expressed much anxiety to be relieved, being

SECT. 7. apprehensive of an attack from the Caribs, who had assembled in considerable numbers on the heights about it. They were much distressed for provisions, and had very little ammunition. Notwithstanding Marinier had capitulated for all the Republican troops, yet two companies contrived to escape from the Vigie, pending the negociation; the Brigands on their retreat to Mount William, wantonly destroyed the extensive sugar works on Colonarie Vale, thus manifesting their perfidious disposition and enmity towards the English; these buildings had twice been in possession of the enemy during the Insurrection, and were retaken uninjured. It was singularly hard on the proprietors to sustain such a loss at the conclusion of their disasters.

Caribs retreat.

The Caribs at length reduced to their own resources, seemed disposed to discontinue hostilities for the future. On the 15th, they sent in a flag of truce to Mount Young, proposing an accommodation; three Chiefs, Desfon, Jack Gordon and Baptiste, were accordingly conducted to town by the Dragoons, where they received their answer, and returned the following day; with singular modesty they proposed a reconciliation on the basis of retaining their lands; they observed, " They had burned the English houses and cane fields, who in return had burned their canoes, and destroyed their provisions, therefore, on the principle of retaliation, there was no just cause of complaint, or any plausible pretext for continuing the war." On being asked whether they or the English were chargeable with the first violation of that treaty of friendship and good neighbourhood, which had subsisted between them, they replied, they had first declared war, but of what were they guilty in consequence? every body was then at war. In reply to the proposals of these misguided men, they were given to understand that there was no room for negociation, that nothing short of unconditional submission would be attended to, in which case their lives would be spared, and they would be treated with humanity; should they refuse this unmerited extension of benignity, the whole force of the Island, would be employed against them, and their extirpation must be the consequence; they remonstrated strongly against such an apparently cruel and arbitrary decision, they could not, they said, recollect any

SECT. 7. thing in their behaviour that could render them obnoxious to the inhabitants, but since absolute necessity required acquiescence on their part, they requested until the 18th, to consult with the Chiefs of families, on which day they would return and give a definite answer.

It was utterly impossible for the English to come again to any terms of accommodation with these perfidious and deceitful people; it was a principle of their religion to wage inexpiable war, and such was their attachment to their old, and inseparable allies, the French, that they were ever ready to co-operate with them in any acts of sanguinary vengeance. In 1769, they volunteered to Count D'Ennery, then Governor of Martinico, to extirpate the English inhabitants with very little assistance from him, but that nobleman, shocked at such a savage proposal, immediately informed the Colonial Government, and enabled them to take steps to prevent its execution. Victor Hugues however thought and acted differently, he encouraged their ferocious disposition, and excited them to massacre the inhabitants without the slightest provocation, fixing on the night of the festival of Saint Patrick for the deed, when the inhabitants would probably be off their guard; the cruelties that were afterwards perpetrated, the property that was consigned to destruction, clearly proved that no peace could be maintained with these black Caribs. For these reasons the Committee of the Planters had instructed their European Agents to declare, that the one or the other must be removed from the Island,* and it was on this basis that the Governor and Council acted in the present emergency; the Government, having viewed the subject in the same light, were convinced of the propriety of such a resolution, and in consequence directed the removal of the Caribs to Rattan, a small island in the Bay of Honduras.†

* See the Memorial in the Appendix, No. XV.

† The Colonists of Jamaica acted upon the same principles of self defence, in 1796, they removed the Maroon negroes, (so called from the Spanish, Cimarron.) As the two cases are very similar, a short abstract of the history of this people will not be deemed irrelevant.

When Jamaica was taken from the Spaniards in 1655, they possessed about one thousand five hundred African slaves, who on the surrender of their masters, retreated to the mountains, and kept up a petty warfare on the English.

SECT. 7.   When the time for their answer had expired, the Caribs disappeared from Mount Young; but as no hostile measures were taken against them, they soon returned and commenced trafficking in their usual manner; their canoes however were effectually secured, but owing to injudicious delays, nothing further was done towards their subjugation, except a few parties of the Rangers scouring the country in search of Brigands, and discovering camps in different parts of the Island.

The Governor issued a Proclamation on the 24th June, declaring martial law at an end;

In 1738, they obtained peace, and one thousand five hundred acres of land were assigned to one body of them at Trelawney; others had lands given them at other places. By this Treaty the Maroons were declared free, with liberty to enjoy their lands, and live within their bounds; Governors over them, named by the Governor, were appointed. In 1795, a revolt took place; after a severe struggle, which lasted nearly a year, they again submitted, but many did not surrender within the prescribed period, and in consequence about six hundred were shipped, in June 1796, for Halifax, Nova Scotia, and twenty-five thousand pounds was appropriated by the Legislature for the purchase of lands, and forming a settlement for them; they have since been removed to Sierra Leone.—See Bryan Edwards, Vol. I. p. 573, and the Jamaica Law Report, page 125.

and on the 13th July, a Colonial Assembly was summoned. Previous to this, the inhabitants held a general meeting with the Governor to discuss the measures proper to be adopted towards the Caribs, when it was proposed that the small Island of Balliceaux (a corruption of petit l'isle oiseaux) should be appropriated for their temporary reception, until the intentions of Government could be ascertained, the proprietor, Mr. Campbell, cheerfully giving it up for this purpose.* This was communicated to General Abercromby, who issued orders on the 15th of July, for the removal of the Caribs to this Island. Pursuant to these instructions, General Hunter required the immediate attendance of the Chiefs, several were accordingly escorted to Kingstown, and given to understand that they were to be removed to Balliceaux, where they would be supplied with a sufficient quantity of provisions and water for their support, and in their ultimate removal be furnished with every convenience necessary, and essential to their future existence; four days were given

* He was afterwards indemnified for the losses he sustained on this occasion, by the Colony; the compensation he received in 1797, was £1731. 15s. currency.

them to take their resolution, at which time in case of non-compliance, hostilities were to commence against them. During this interval many of the Chiefs frequently resorted to the camp, and gave the most specious promises of complying with the orders which they had received from General Hunter. On the 16th and 17th, a considerable number of Caribs exceeding six hundred, came from their camp in the heights, and took a position between the English posts and the sea, at about half a mile distance from Mount William. The Chiefs and heads of families were detached with the information, that in consequence of being daily harassed by parties of the Rangers and other troops, they wished to place themselves under English protection, until they could comply with the orders of the Commander-in-Chief, which they all repeatedly promised to do.

The following day, the son of Chatoyer, in the presence of Lieutenant-Colonel Haffey and his officers, addressed himself to the attendant Caribs, to the following effect; " It is no disgrace to us to surrender to a great nation, the subjects of France and all great nations, even of England, are obliged to submit to each

other, when there no longer remains the means
of resistance. What else is now left for us ? have
we power to continue the war ? No! to-morrow
morning I will set you the example of submission, by bringing my family to Colonel Haffey,
that he may send us to the General, you may
do as you please, I can only be accountable for
myself and my family." These observations
seemingly had the effect he pretended to desire,
and the Caribs universally promised with the
most energetic asseverations, to accompany him.
But being too well acquainted with their perfidy, not to entertain strong doubts of their
compliance with their promises, Colonel Haffey
on the next day ordered his corps under arms,
and sent Captain Lauder with two companies
to line the deep ravine to the northward of
them, Captain Munro with two others, to the
southern ridge, himself occupying a post to the
westward. When Captain Lauder had made
the necessary arrangements, he proceeded alone
to prevent alarm, and to persuade the Caribs to
submit, but he found their numbers very much
reduced, for upwards of three hundred had fled
to their retreat in the woods, and among the
number, was the orator Chatoyer himself, and

SECT. 7. all of those who had been most liberal in their promises of submission. Captain Munro in closing with the enemy's camp, took one hundred and two of them who were retreating towards Colonarie, who with the others that were that day made prisoners, amounted to two hundred and eighty men; on the 20th, they were conducted to Calliaqua, and after-

Their Removal to Balliceaux. wards transported to Balliceaux, but instead of voluntary captives they owed their situation more to the judicious precautions that were taken against them, than to any regard for their treaties or promises of surrender.

The same day Lieutenant Laborde of the Rangers was detached to Grand Sable, with a party of about thirty men, to receive the proffered submission of the Caribs in that quarter, and conduct them to Mount Young; on his arrival, he found their houses abandoned, and themselves under arms, to the number of two hundred, in possession of a convenient little eminence from whence they called to him, and ordered him to withdraw immediately, declaring at the same time, that they never would submit to the English, and they did not revolt so much from the prospect of death, as from the idea of submission. The inferiority of his force, rendered his retreat both prudent and necessary. Much about the same hour, a detachment of men under the command of Lieutenant-Colonel Graham,* having pursued the line formed by the bed of Colonarie River to a considerable elevation, discovered a large party of the enemy, strongly fortified; they invited him to approach with the utmost seeming sincerity of friendship, which he did at the head of his men, displaying a white handkerchief in his hand, indicative of his pacific disposition; this officer had frequently expressed his good opinion of the Caribs, and of their similar dispositions towards him; but when he had got within a few yards of their works, a whole volley of musketry was poured around him, and severely wounded him and an officer of Santeurs' corps, and all his party, except Mr. Matthews their guide; the latter officer fell into the possession of the Caribs, who cut him in pieces.

* Samuel Graham became Lieutenant-General in 1814, the wounds that this officer received were most severe, and his recovery miraculous.—See a particular account of his services in Stewart's History of the Highland Regiments, Vol. I. p. 433.

SECT. 7.   After this the troops retreated, various skirmishes frequently ensued ; more than one thousand houses were devoted to the flames in a few
days, the natural consequence of endeavours to
destroy the property of the enemy, and sundry
canoes of very large dimensions were also
burned. Lieutenant-Colonel Haffey's Rangers
fell in with a camp about four miles above
Rabacca, which they carried with some loss,
Lieutenant M'Kenzie being severely wounded ;
they afterwards attacked a camp on the heights
above Grand Sable, which after a protracted
resistance, principally arising from the ex-
cellence of the situation, was carried with the
loss of five killed and twenty-three wounded.

On the 6th of August, a party of Brigands
and negroes belonging to French inhabitants,
attacked Mr. Gorst's Plantation in Layou, and
carried off him and his overseer Mr. Robert
Haus, the latter escaped, and the party soon
released Mr. Gorst, carrying away with them
every thing they could find in the house ; these
persons were ascertained to be part of those
that escaped from the Vigie during the truce,
and were under the command of Marin Pedre,
a black from Saint Lucia, whom they had left

five days before in the heights above Colonarie. SECT. 7.
On the 8th, Lieutenant Burton of the 63d,
with fifty Regulars from Greig's Ridge*, being
joined by Farquhar Campbell and Robert
Sutherland,† Esqs. marched through Benny and
Davis' lands, until they fell in with Kennedy's
Trace, which they pursued westward, until
they came to the Ridge, which divides Charlotte Parish from Saint George's, where they
discovered a path leading to the mountains,
and after a progress of three miles, they saw a
camp, but on a shot having been prematurely
fired, about forty persons made their escape,
leaving one killed and two prisoners. Lieutenant-Colonel Abercromby established himself
at Duvallé's Settlement, which he found abandoned. Letraille, Delaprade and Jean Toulie,
noted characters, surrendered themselves.

At length two prisoners were brought over
from Balliceaux, and sent into the woods to
report to their countrymen the treatment of

---

* Sir John Wardlaw, Bart. a Colonel in 1814, commanded this post.

† Robert Sutherland, one of the first Settlers in the Carib
Lands, died October, 1828, and Farquhar Campbell, December, 1829.

SECT. 7. their friends in captivity, this was attended with the happiest consequences, as not a day passed without some persons coming in; but a desperate party under Hippolite attacked the post at Turama, defended by Major Brown of the 40th, with one hundred and fifty of his men, and after three assaults, in which they were repulsed, they retired leaving their commander and two others killed, close to the breast-work.

The whole of September was passed in these continual efforts to surprise and capture the straggling parties of the enemy, and to destroy their provision grounds, in which the Rangers distinguished themselves by their unceasing activity and perseverance; the good effects of this system of warfare were soon apparent, the enemy were compelled to retreat more and more into the interior, and the circle of their excursions and territories was consequently much circumscribed. A party of Rangers ascended the Souffriere on the leeward side, and after much difficulty succeeded in passing over it and descending by the bed of the Rabacca River, which had a considerable effect on the enemy, and convinced them that they might

Exertions of the Rangers,

be approached in all directions. On the 2d of October, Marin Pedre attended by Moniquet, and a few others, came to the advanced post above Rabacca, and surrendered himself to Captain M'Murdoch of the Buffs, who conducted him to Lieutenant-Colonel Smollet*, who commanded at Mount Young, when being perfectly satisfied with his reception, and the assurances of security to all those who would follow his example, he dispatched messengers to the different parties, and in consequence several hundred persons of all descriptions sur- rendered; among the Chiefs, Thunder, Toussaint and Emanuel, were the most prominent characters, and soon after Duvallé and young Chatoyer, were added to the number. On the 26th of October the numbers that had sur-

---

* Besides the officers already named, the following also, were with the army, in different situations. Archibald Campbell, Lieutenant-General 1811; Robert Lethbridge, Sir Thomas Brisbane, Major Generals 1813; Lewis Mosheim, Sir Henry Torrens, (died 1829) Major Generals 1814; Sir C. P. Belson, W. A. Prevost, John Locke, Major Generals 1819; David Stewart, Major General 1825, (died 1829;) B. Wynne Ottley, George Mackie, Colonels 1814; William Fenwick, Lieutenant-Colonel 1808; John Mansel, Lieutenant-Colonel 1812.

SECT. 7. rendered amounted to five thousand and eighty; men, women and children ; they were supplied with provisions by the Colony, and on the 25th of February, 1797, His Majesty's ship Experiment, Captain Barrett, arrived from Martinico with transports to carry the Caribs to Rattan.* They were embarked from Bequia, where the transports lay, and on the 11th of March,

Removal to Rattan. sailed for their place of destination. They were landed with some opposition on the part of the Spaniards, who had constructed a fort, from whence Captain Barrett found it was necessary to dislodge them, and which he left the Caribs in possession of; in executing this service he had five men killed and five wounded. Major-General Hunter and Captain Barrett both received addresses from the Colonial Legislature for their distinguished efforts in this eventful struggle, with the present of a sword

* Baron Humboldt in his personal Narrative, Vol. VI. p. 32, says, " These unhappy remains of a people heretofore powerful, were banished because they were *accused* by the English Government of having connexions with the French." Should the learned foreigner ever meet with this humble narrative, he will be enabled to give a better reason for the punishment inflicted on them.

to each.   It was also resolved to erect a monument to the memory of such inhabitants as
had fallen in defence of the Island, at the public
expence, which unfortunately has never been
carried into effect.

The expences of the hire of negroes to form
the corps of Rangers, with their loss, and the
hire of mules and cattle, as established before
the Committee appointed to investigate the
claims against the Colony, amounted to upwards of fifty-seven thousand pounds sterling;
this however, formed but a small part of the
aggregate loss to the proprietors, for the Committee of expenditure during the Insurrection,
drew bills on His Majesty's Treasury for forty
thousand pounds for the general expences of
the war, which sum was for a long time claimed
from the Colony, by that Board, and it was
not until November, 1807, that Mr. Alexander,
the Treasurer, obtained a Treasury Warrant
to discharge him from that payment, which
seems to have been acceded to from the contemplation of indemnity by the sale of the
Carib Lands.   By an address to His Majesty
on the 15th of May, 1798, praying an extension of time for the repayment of the Exchequer

sect. 7. Loan, the Council and Assembly stated their
expences and losses at a strictly moderate com-
putation, to exceed nine hundred thousand
pounds sterling.

SECTION VIII.

*Re-establishment of Cultivation—Governor William
Bentinck—Carib Occupancies—Carib Settlement
at Morne Ronde—Sir George Beckwith—Colonel
Browne—Sir Charles Brisbane—Eruption of the
Souffriere—Colonial Events—Death of the Go-
vernor.*

THE Island now began to recover slowly from
its disasters, and instead of a connected narrative of military events, the Reader must now
only look for brief disjointed notices of passing
events, which are chronicled more for the sake
of uniformity, than from any interest they can
be expected to excite. Although the war had
terminated, it was necessary to maintain a
corps of Rangers for the purpose of scouring the
woods of the few remaining Caribs who remained encamped there, and they were not
disbanded until 1799; gradually the planters
resumed their natural pursuits, the buildings
on the estates were renewed, and the negroes
returned to the cultivation of the soil; it was
some time however before the excitement pro-

SECT. 8. duced by the war, could be subdued, or the uniform tenor of peace be enjoyed by the inhabitants, their expenditure had been immense, and they were ill prepared to raise the requisite means for the re-establishment of their properties ; in this emergency, application was made to the Parliament to relieve them by a loan of Exchequer Bills which was favourably attended to.

In June 1797, Governor Seton expressed his intention of retiring from the fatigues of office, in consequence of old age, and an address commemorative of his valuable services to the colony, was voted to him by the Council and Governor Assembly. He was succeeded by William William Bentinck, Esquire, who arrived in the Colony, the 28th of February, 1798.

The inhabitants now began to look around them for an indemnity for their disasters occasioned by the Caribs, and as those fertile plains, extending from Mount Young to the termination of the plain northward by some deep ravines, which in 1771, had excited the cupidity of the first settlers, were now desolate and without an owner, the Assembly resolved to apply to the Government for a sale of them, and a bill was brought in for the purpose of causing a survey to be made, but some obstacles interposed, and no further proceedings were adopted at this period. The ever sanguine disposition of the Planters had over rated their abilities to repay the Exchequer loan within the proposed time, and an address to His Majesty for an extension of time for repayment was presented in 1798. Resolutions were also entered into for the building the Court House and Gaol.

It was in this year that Mr. Samuel Clapham, a part owner of Mount William Estate, was murdered by some Caribs, with every circumstance of savage ferocity, near the Rabacca River, where he had gone on a fishing excursion, and by an unaccountable neglect, or impossibility, the perpetrators were not brought to punishment. Several desperate characters by this time had surrendered themselves, or had been collected from the woods who were afterwards directed by the British Government to be removed to the Spanish Main, among others the notorious Cuffy Wilson, who was tried and sentenced to be executed, but it appearing that he had saved the lives of Captain

N

SECT. 8. M'Cumming, and other prisoners, the sentence was commuted to banishment.

The forts of the Island were again ordered to be repaired, the Government undertaking to supply guns, carriages, and materials, but the labour of transport and construction was to be defrayed by the Colony. The Government was several times administered by Drewry Ottley, the President of the Council, during the nomination of this Governor, with such ability, that a piece of plate of the value of three hundred guineas was voted to him.

Carib Oc-
cupancies.
On the 11th June, 1802, Henry William Bentinck, Esquire, who had been appointed Governor, arrived; he granted occupancies or possessions during His Majesty's pleasure, of five thousand two hundred and sixty-two acres of the Carib lands to different persons, who had been actually engaged in the war, and a new field for industry and exertion was soon displayed. An act was passed in June 1804, declaring that by the late rebellion, the Caribs had forfeited all claim to their lands, under the treaty of 1773, and that they were consequently re-vested in the crown. The remaining Caribs after nearly eight years experience,

not having shewn any disposition to excite further disturbances, were pardoned by an act of May 1805, on condition of surrender and submission to the laws; but it was expressly stated, that no right to any of the lands formerly occupied by them, was recognised. They were situated at Morne Ronde, where an oc- cupancy of two hundred and thirty acres of land was granted for their subsistence, which they were prohibited from alienating, or cultivating in sugar. This was strongly opposed by the Council and Assembly, and the Governor was earnestly requested to cause them to be removed from the Colony. Their fears in this instance appear to have been premature; the Caribs remain there in peace and idleness, except a few who emigrated to Trinidad in 1812, being terrified at the eruption of the Souffriere; their employments are the making canoes, baskets, and fish pots, and on the windward coast they are sometimes useful in rough weather in assisting to ship the sugars from such of the estates, as are not provided with wharfs and cranes, for their habits are so amphibious, that they have acquired great dexterity in this application of their labour.

sect. 8. But such is their natural indolence, they can seldom be roused to exertion for any continued period, unless it be to obtain a supply of rum, which is their chief enjoyment.

Mr. Ottley, who again administered the Government in this year, died while in office, and was succeeded by Robert Paul, Esq. the next senior member of the Council.

Sir George Beckwith.

Sir George Beckwith * was appointed to the Government in 1804, but did not arrive in the West Indies until 1805, when the command of the forces devolved on him in consequence of the death of Sir William Myers, and it was not until 1806, that he resumed his station at Saint Vincent.

Colonel Browne.

Colonel Thomas Browne, an English gentleman, who had established a settlement at Augusta, in Georgia, in the commencement of the American war of independence, adhered to his Sovereign, and obtained the command of some irregular troops, with which he distin-

* Sir George Beckwith died March 1823, aged seventy years, he had been Governor of Bermuda in 1797, and of Barbados from 1808 to 1814, his abilities, independence, and integrity, have never been surpassed, and are universally acknowledged by the Colonists

guished himself on many occasions; he was also superintendant of the different tribes of Indians attached to the English army. At the close of the contest, he retired to the Caycos in the Bahama Islands, but finding the lands there to be exhausted, and dreading the proximity of St. Domingo, he was enabled to obtain from the British Government, as a remuneration for his acknowledged services, a promise of a grant of six thousand acres of the Carib lands. This alarmed the occupants, who had gradually cleared their lands, and which were in a progressive state of improvement and cultivation. Petitions were presented to the Council and Assembly against the measure being carried into effect, which were forwarded to the Colonial office; the impolicy of such an enormous grant to one individual, was strongly insisted on, from the impossibility of his being able to carry on the cultivation so extensively, as if it remained in the present settlements, consequently the injury to the revenue, and the loss to the Colony would be immense. Fortunately for the occupants, they employed the late Dr. Colquhoun as their agent, who by his unremitting exertions succeeded in shewing the

SECT. 8. impolicy of the grant, and being authorised to offer a certain sum for the purchase of the lands, the Government was induced to pause.   Previous to this the occupants had offered to purchase their tenements of Colonel Browne, at twenty pounds per acre, or to cultivate under lease from him, being unwilling to lose the labour they had expended in clearing the lands, and justly priding themselves on the possession of what they had obtained by their valour, but he refused; during a long and protracted discussion of claims and counter claims, which lasted until the year 1809, an unfortunate act of misconduct on the part of the Colonel occurred, which alienated the liberal views of His Majesty's Government from him; he obtained one thousand seven hundred acres, the remainder was sold to the occupants at the rate of twenty-two pounds ten shillings per acre of cleared land, except in some cases, where grants were made for the benefit of the families of individuals who had suffered in the war.   Colonel Browne received a part of this money, amounting to about twenty-five thousand pounds, the remainder was at the disposal of Government; by this judicious arrangement

the land was divided into eight large estates,
the different claimants were apparently satisfied,
and a great and permanent increase of the
revenue has been secured.

Sir George Beckwith having been appointed
Governor of Barbados, Sir Charles Brisbane, a
Captain in the navy, who had recently signa-
lized himself in the capture of the Dutch Island
of Curáçao, was named as his successor on the
14th of November, 1808, and arrived in the
Colony in January following.

A French Planter of the name of St. Hilaire,
who resided alone in a small Island called
Myera, was murdered by his own slaves while
working in the fields, and so indifferent, or
ignorant were they, that they took no precautions for their escape; on the arrival of his
brother from a neighbouring Island, he soon
learned the dreadful event from some of the
domestics, but maintained sufficient presence
of mind to appear ignorant of the real case,
pretending to expect his brother's return; the
next morning he ordered the people into the
cotton house, on their usual avocations, and
assisted by his own servant, actually seized
and bound the principal persons he suspected;

SECT. 8. some of the women gave evidence against the perpetrators of this foul deed, and five were convicted, of whom the principal was executed at Myera, and four in Kingstown.

Eruption of the Souffriere. The following years passed on without any particular occurrences until 1812, when the dreadful eruption of the Souffriere took place; this mountain is situated at the northern extremity of the Island, and is the last of a chain, which was called Morne a Garou by the natives, and is about three thousand feet above the level of the sea. Baron Humboldt states in his personal Narrative that it had thrown out flames in 1718, but from whence his information was derived has not been satisfactorily ascertained, but that there had been previous eruptions, either from this, or some other source, the volcanic formation of the whole Island, and the different strata of which all the mountains are composed, sufficiently indicate, and it appears probable from the events that occurred on the main land, that some subterraneous communication exists with the continent. After various oscillations of the earth, a dreadful earthquake happened at the Caraccas in March, which destroyed the whole of that City, and nine thousand persons lost their lives; the Vallies of the Mississippi and the Ohio, were at the same time in a state of commotion; and thirty-two days afterwards, on the 27th of April, the eruption burst forth.

Previous to this event, according to the best accounts, which are here consolidated, the appearance of this mountain was singularly romantic, the crater was half a mile in diameter, and five hundred feet in depth; in the centre of this hollow was a conical hill, two hundred feet in diameter, and three hundred in heighth, the lower half of which was fringed with brushwood, shrubs and vines, while the upper was strewed with virgin sulphur, at the base of it were two small lakes, the one sulphureous and aluminous, the other pure and tasteless; from the fissures of the cone a thin white smoke exuded, occasionally tinged with a light blue flame. Evergreens, flowers, aromatic shrubs, and many alpine plants clothed the steep sides of the crater, and from its external base, nearly to the summit; the mountain was covered with an exuberant growth of forest trees.

The first indication was a severe concussion of the earth, a tremulous noise in the air, and

SECT. 8. the bursting forth of a vast column of thick black smoke from the crater. Volumes of sand and favillæ darkened the air like a heavy storm of rain, and covered the woods, ridges and cane pieces, with light grey ashes, resembling snow thinly strewed with dust, which speedily destroyed every appearance of vegetation; for three days all these symptoms continued to increase; during this the sun seemed to be in a total eclipse, the sea was discoloured, the ground bore a wintry appearance from the thick crust of the fallen ashes, and the cattle were starving for the want of their accustomed food.

On the 30th at noon, the column of smoke assumed a sanguine hue, rose with a livelier motion, and dilated itself more extensively, the noise became incessant with a vibration that affected the feelings and hearing; the Caribs who were resident at Morne Ronde, fled from their houses to Kingstown, and the negroes from their work, and the very birds were beaten to the earth overpowered by the sand and stones projected from the mountain; at length, just as the day closed the flame burst forth pyramidically from the crater, the thunder now grew deafening, and electric flashes, some like rockets, and some like shells darting in all directions, and in all forms, illumined the immense column of smoke, which hung over the volcano. In a short time the lava poured out on the north west side, it was opposed there by the acclivity of a higher point of land, but being driven on by fresh accessions, it ascended and surmounted the obstacle, forming the figure V in a torrent of fire, plunged over the cliff, carrying down rocks and woods in its course, and finally precipitating itself into a vast ravine at the foot of Morne Ronde; all this while large globular bodies of fire were exploded from the crater, which burst, and either fell back into it, or among the surrounding bushes, which were instantly in a blaze; in about four hours the torrent of lava reached the sea, and shortly after, another stream descended eastward towards Rabacca. The Island was now shaken by an earthquake, it was followed by a shower of cinders which fell like hail for two hours, and this was followed by a fall of stones mingled with fire, which continued for an hour. Many houses were set on fire, many negroes were wounded, and some

SECT. 8. were killed, but happily the weight of the stones bore no proportion to their magnitude, or the sufferers from them would have been still more numerous than they were. At length in the afternoon of the 1st of May, the eruption ceased, and the mountain sunk gradually into a solemn silence: the volcano however still burned, and on the 9th of June, it again gave alarming signs of activity, but nothing more occurred than the throwing up of a quantity of stones and ashes, which fell back into the abyss, from whence they came.

All the former beauty of the Souffriere, was of course destroyed, the conical mount disappeared, and an extensive lake of yellow coloured water, whose agitated waves perpetually threw up vast quantities of black sand, supplied its place. A new crater was formed on the north east of the original one, and the face of the mountain was entirely changed; many of the adjoining ravines were filled up, particularly Wallibo and Duvallé's, in the former the river was absorbed for some years, but the gradual accumulation of water burst through the sandy barrier, and carried away many negro houses in its progress; thirty-two slaves belonging to Wallibo Estate, were washed into the sea by the torrent.

At Duvallé's, the former settlement of the Carib Chief, a sugar plantation had been established by Messieurs Thesiger and Calvelly, the works, situated in a valley were entirely covered by the sand and ashes, and some hogsheads of sugar remain there at present calcined to a cinder. The Rabacca river was also filled up, and its stream seldom reaches the sea except in cases of heavy rains.

It was at first feared that the Island would be rendered barren by the ashes which lay on its surface to a considerable depth, but they did not prove so injurious as was supposed. The great danger was famine; but the neighbouring Colonies of Barbados, Demerary and Dominica, with a generous promptitude hastened to supply the Island with provisions, and a Committee was appointed by the Council and Assembly for the purpose of purchasing supplies. An investigation of the losses sustained was also made, and a petition presented to the Prince Regent, praying for relief, which was most favourably received, and on the case being laid before Parliament, the sum of twenty-

sect. 8. five thousand pounds, was voted for the relief of the sufferers.*

It is a wonderful circumstance although the air was perfectly calm during the eruption, that Barbados which is eighty miles to the windward, was covered several inches deep with the ashes, and the inhabitants on the last day of the eruption, were terrified by the approach of utter darkness which continued for four hours and a half, and then slowly decreased; there also, and in several other Islands, the troops were under arms, supposing from the continued noise, that the hostile fleets were engaging.

Colonial
Events.

Sir Charles Brisbane having sailed for England on some circumstance connected with the appropriation of the Carib lands, he took the opportunity of representing to Mr. Perceval, who then held the office of Prime Minister, the propriety of appropriating at least a part of the purchase money towards the building a church in Kingstown, when the sum of five thousand pounds sterling was promised, and afterwards paid.

On the insurrection in Barbados in April

* See the Appendix, No. XVII.

1816, it was deemed prudent to place the Island under martial law, which was continued only for a short time; neither on this, or on any other occasion, has the slave population of Saint Vincent ever manifested a disposition to enter into political questions, or to claim fancied rights, a certain sign of contentment in their station.   While slavery exists, it is no doubt an evil, but the most prejudiced Abolitionist must admit that it exists in this Island in a very mitigated form.

No colonial events appear worthy of record, except a severe hurricane in 1819, which here however only caused some slight injury to the crop on the ground, but its fury was expended on the neighbouring Islands, where great damage was sustained.

On the removal of the commercial restrictions imposed on the American Trade, her flag made its appearance in the ports of the West Indies, in 1822, and the supplies of lumber and provisions became more abundant; but the demand for colonial produce not being so great, a proportion of the payments were made in specie, to the great inconvenience of the in-

SECT. 8. habitants, from the loss of the circulating medium; this intercourse however soon ceased.

On the 13th October, 1824, the Colony was thrown into consternation by the murder of Major Champion, who commanded a part of the twenty-first regiment stationed at Fort Charlotte; a private named Ballasty, who was posted as sentry at the drawbridge, having previously determined to carry his diabolical design into execution, loaded his musket with ball, and challenged the Major on his return from an evening ride; on receiving an answer in the affirmative, he deliberately fired and shot him through the body, the unfortunate Officer survived only a few hours; the Governor with his usual promptness and decision, summoned a Special Court of Sessions, when the assassin was tried, convicted, and executed on the draw-bridge, where the crime had been committed.

In consequence of the appointment of a Bishop to the Diocese of Barbados and the Leeward Islands, Saint Vincent was honoured with a first visitation in April 1825, to the great satisfaction of all classes, and to the wonder of the negroes.

In November 1829, Sir Charles Brisbane sect. 8. died, having administered the Government for Death of the unprecedented period of twenty years, with the Governor. great satisfaction; he experienced a steady support from all the different Administrations under whose orders he executed the Commands of His Majesty, and his occasional political differences in the Colony were either so trifling, or so soon subsided, that few Islands have been able to boast of such a lengthened period of tranquillity, so pleasing and beneficial to the inhabitants.

SECTION IX.

*Form of the present Government—Courts of Justice—
Slave Laws—Registry Acts—Commerce—Ecclesiastical Establishment—Education—Colonial Deficiencies.*

THE authorities which constitute the Government of the Island, are, the Governor, Council,
and Assembly, the former is appointed by His
Majesty's Letters Patent, he is Chancellor and
Ordinary under the same instrument, and Vice
Admiral under a commission from the Lords
of the Admiralty. His duties are regulated by
instructions from His Majesty, which are said
to have been originally framed in the time of
Charles II. for the Island of Jamaica, and have
been adopted for the other Islands; to these
may be added His Majesty's Proclamation of
the 7th of October, 1763, which may be called
the foundation of the insular constitution, by
this authority the general assemblies are summoned, and the powers of enacting laws, as
near as may be to the laws of England, are
given, the authority for erecting Courts of

Judicature, with the liberty of appeal, is also recognised in this document, which was promulgated after the treaty of Paris. The Governor's salary, which he is required by his instructions, to apply for on his first meeting the Council and Assembly, is four thousand pounds currency.*

The Council consists of twelve Members, five or six of whom are usually named in the Governor's Commission, and the remainder supplied by recommendation of the Governor, or by mandamus; five in number constitute a board, and when the original number is reduced to seven, the Governor has a power of nomination to supply the vacancies. By a late rule of the Colonial Office, no Councillor can be absent longer than twelve months, after that period his name is directed to be struck out, but no objection appears to his readmission at a subsequent period as the junior member; the Council sit in two capacities, Privy and Legislative, in the former the Governor pre-

---

* From particular circumstances Sir Charles Brisbane after some years residence, obtained an increase, and in consequence of the dilapidated state of the Government House, an allowance was made him for house rent.

SECT. 9. sides, in the latter the senior member, under the title of President, on whom also the temporary Government devolves on the absence, or death of a Governor. Since the appointment of a Bishop, he has been sworn in ex-officio a Member of Council in all the Islands composing his diocese, and where the date of his appointment has preceded that of a Governor, he is also Ordinary.

The Assembly consists of nineteen members, three for each of the five parishes, two for the town of Kingstown, and the like number for the Grenadines; the qualification of Members for the Parishes and Islands, is fifty acres of land in cultivation, or producing an income of three hundred pounds currency a year, and for the town a house of the yearly value of one hundred pounds; the titles of the candidates to their property must appear to have been registered in the office twelve months, except in cases of wills, and conveyances of property executed in Great Britain. Electors must have a freehold of ten acres, or a house in Kingstown of twenty pounds yearly value, or of ten pounds elsewhere, registered in like manner. Elections take place under the authority of a

writ issuing from the Governor and Council,
on an application from the Speaker, to the
Provost Marshal General, and the whole regulations, on this subject, are prescribed by an
Act of the Legislature, which passed in 1786;
these three branches assimilate their proceedings as near as possible to those of Great Britain; their meetings are quarterly, and the
Acts that are passed are proclaimed by the
Marshal, and enrolled in the Register's Office.
These Acts may be divided into three classes,
the first temporary and purely colonial, which
take effect immediately on their publication;
the second, such as have a clause annexed suspending their operation until His Majesty's
pleasure be known; and the third, the permanent laws, which if not confirmed in two years
from their enactment, are to be considered as
disallowed. In strictness the Governor is not
authorised to pass any law, repealing one
which may have received the royal approbation,
without a suspending clause; but this in the
cases of the old laws, has been frequently overlooked. The Attorney General has a salary of
five hundred pounds currency per annum, which
is in part given to him for framing the bills,

SECT. 9. which any member may require, but he is not obliged to introduce them to either house, and a considerable difficulty has frequently occurred from the want of an accredited person, as the organ of Government, who might introduce the measures proposed by the crown through the Colonial Secretary, to either house. At present the Governor communicates by letters with the President and Speaker, but no member is intrusted with the charge of carrying any bills through the different stages prescribed by the Legislature.

Courts of Justice.   The supreme court for civil causes is called the Court of King's Bench and Common Pleas, where the Chief Justice presides ; his salary is two thousand pounds currency. There are three other Assistant Justices, who are not professional persons, and act without any salary. This Court holds its sittings for the trial of causes once in the month, from March to August, when executions for debts can be obtained in about ten weeks, from the entering day. The proceedings are regulated by a Court Act. The Court of Sessions for the trial of criminal offences is held twice a year. The Chief Justice is President, and the Members of

Council and Judges sit according to seniority. sect. 9. The Court of Error for appeals from the King's Bench and Common Pleas, is composed of the Governor and Council. The Governor is also sole Chancellor, and from these two last courts an appeal lies to His Majesty in Council. In consequence of the reports of the Commissioners of legal enquiry, it may be fully expected that the whole judicial system of the West Indies, will be greatly modified, and improved, for the defects of the present, must be obvious to the most superficial observer.

The government of the slave population, is chiefly under the control of the Magistrates, except in specified cases; two Justices sit in rotation at the Court House in Kingstown, twice in each month, to hear and determine all petty offences; the punishments of slaves are regulated by a Slave Act, and recently, since the establishment of a treadmill, by the laws regulating the same. The old Slave Act of 1768, having been deemed inappropriate to the improved condition of the negroes, after several partial amendments, and particularly by an Act passed in 1813, which gave slaves the advantage of a trial by jury, the same as free

Slave Laws.

sect. 9. persons in all capital offences, with the additional benefit of being defended by Counsel ;*
it was entirely repealed in 1820, and has been
re-enacted every seven years, with gradual concessions and improvements according to the
progress of civilization, but the advocates
against slavery are too sanguine in their expectation, and press what they deem improvements too rapidly on the Colonists, who in this
case at least, must be the best judges of the
state of that society in which they are domi-
ciled, and what concessions may be really
advantageous to them.

There are two principal points to be considered in this long agitated question, the
rights of the owner, and the amelioration of
the slave; both these are distinctly admitted
in the celebrated parliamentary resolutions of
1823. As the Planters have not done that
species of wrong, which is to exclude them
from full compensation for their rights, if the
Government in compliance with the improved

* This Act was introduced by Mr. Sharpe, late Chief
Justice of the Colony, and will ever remain a conspicuous
monument of his humanity as a man, and sound judgment
as a lawyer.

state of the world, is disposed to abolish the sect. 9. system, it can only in justice be done on this principle.* But then secondly, when the slaves are made free, what is to become of them? the great mass is not yet qualified to receive this concession with advantage, they will perish from the want of that support which they now derive from their masters; the superior classes, such as Carpenters, Masons, and Coopers, may perhaps work, if their services should be sought after in the proposed new state of freedom, which is doubtful; but the field negroe, when free, will never be induced by any remuneration to cultivate the soil as a permanent employment, and as a necessary consequence, the manufacture of sugar will cease in the West Indian Islands.† A more

* See Lord Stowell's elaborate judgment in the Case of the Slave, Grace, where he forcibly illustrates this doctrine.

† The able and judicious Notes on Haiti, by Mr. M'Kenzie, afford a melancholy confirmation of this fact; the negroes in St. Domingo, when compulsion, under the code rural, does not restrain them, have retreated to the woods, they barely till the earth sufficient for their subsistence, and there is no voluntary cultivation of the cane, except to make taffia, or rum, to enable them to indulge in their luxury of intoxication.

sect. 9. extended civilization by means of schools and religious instructors, must be persevered in before any benefit can be derived to the great body of slaves by indiscriminate freedom.

As the slave code of St. Vincent has had the good fortune to obtain (with some very trifling exceptions) the approbation of His Majesty, an abstract of it is inserted in the Appendix.

Registry Acts.   It having been deemed expedient by the Government, to establish a registry of slaves, the Legislature of the Colony passed an Act in 1817, by which the names, ages, and descriptions of all slaves were enrolled; these returns are renewed every three years, and copies of the books are sent to the General Registry Establishment in London, at a considerable expence. After eleven years experience, it may be safely averred, that not a single advantage either to the master or to the slave, has yet been derived from it. The statistical knowledge it affords was previously obtained by other returns, and as the transfer of all pro-

Also the Narrative entitled " Marly," which is the most faithful description of sugar cultivation, and slave management yet published, expresses the same idea, p. 212.

perty of this kind must be recorded in the Register's Office, the titles are neither confirmed
nor improved. It has established an office of
permanent expence to the Colony, without being
productive of any benefit, and is another striking
example of the inutility of theory, in the principles of legislation.*

The Police cf the Island has been greatly
improved of late years, and especially in the
town of Kingstown; this is regulated by three
Town Wardens who are annually appointed,
and an Act authorising the appointment of a
Chief Constable, with very extensive powers,
has added materially to the apprehension of
offenders, and the tread-mill affords a mode of

---

* When the Settlements of North and South Carolina
were first established, the celebrated Mr. Locke was applied
to, to form a system of Government, and Codes of Laws for
the new Colonists, but, however wise in theory, these in-
stitutions might have been, it is certain, the Settlement did
not thrive under them; and after some years they were laid
aside. So complicated are human affairs, that it is unsafe
in the formation of political systems, to go far beyond the
line of experience.—See Stedman's History of the American
War, I. 10.; a Work most undeservedly neglected, containing by far the most accurate account of that disastrous
undertaking.

punishment, heretofore unknown. The lower class of persons who occupy the towns are principally seafaring persons, continually changing their residence, and these are little interested in maintaining good order and regularity of conduct, while the cheapness of rum, and the numerous retailers of it, contribute not a little to dissolute habits. In most Islands there are restrictions on strangers arriving or departing, but the extreme severity of the Act, improperly termed the Alien Act (which was passed in 1797, just after the insurrection) prevents the restrictions being carried fully into effect, which if modified, would be very beneficial, and consequently this Island is a place of refuge for a description of persons who in England would immediately be returned to their parishes.

The registration of all real property, in the Register's Office, is requisite, and the deeds of conveyance must be acknowledged either personally, or by Attorney, before the Registrar, he is also Secretary of the Courts, and of the Council, Register in Chancery and Ordinary, and Clerk of the Crown; the office is kept at the Court House. The Provost Marshal General executes an office corresponding to that

of Sheriff, and Inquests are regularly held by SECT. 9.
the Coroner in all necessary cases.

The commerce of the Island is regulated by Commerce.
the officers of His Majesty's Customs, a Col-
lector, Comptroller, and three Waiters constitute the establishment ; the regulations of trade
having been much simplified, and amended of
late years, by the repeal of several hundred Acts,
and consolidating their provisions under six or
eight distinct heads. The fees on shipping are
now abolished, and the salaries of the officers
are defrayed from the dutiable articles imported
from foreign ports, and in cases of deficiency,
bills are drawn on the Treasury of Great Britain.
The variations in the American Trade are so
frequent, that it will be impossible to give any
satisfactory detailed account ; the object of
the British Government has always been to
promote the trade between the British American Settlements, and the West Indies, as
much as possible, but their capabilities of supply
are not at present adequate to the demand, from
a want of capital employed in this branch of
trade ; hence the products of the United States
are introduced to the Colonies under various
subterfuges, either of warehousing in the Ca-

SECT. 9. nadas, or importing from the foreign Islands of St. Thomas or St. Bartholomew. From this source, lumber, staves, shingles, tar, tobacco, &c. are derived, and the returns are made partially only of late years in rum and molasses.* The imports from the French Islands are very limited in value, not so from Great Britain, every article of domestic use and luxury being readily procured here, at a very moderate advance, and the supplies are made with great regularity. The exports to Great Britain, are only the great staple commodities of sugar, rum and molasses, and inconsiderable quantities of arrow root, ginger, coffee, cocoa and turtle-shell. The particulars of the imports and exports are detailed in the Appendix. All breaches of the revenue laws are cognizable in the instance Court of Vice Admiralty, where one Judge presides; the proceeds of the confiscated articles are divided equally between the Crown, the Governor, and seizing officer.

---

* The exports of salt fish, the principal food of the slave population, is confined to the British Colonies, and forms a valuable branch of trade, in which the United States have no participation.

The original Church Establishment, in this, as well as almost all other West India Islands, was miserably defective: the Church in Kings- town having been destroyed in the hurricane of 1780, as before mentioned, the present was finished in 1820, and an Act was passed for the building of Churches in the different parishes. Up to this period, only one has been commenced in Bequia, but the different parishes have been supplied with Ministers who officiate in temporary buildings. The salary of the Rector of Saint George and Saint Andrew, including a compensation for a house and glebe, is one thousand and sixty pounds per annum; the other salaries are seven hundred pounds currency, and the Legislature having resolved on the expenditure of five thousand pounds sterling on ecclesiastical improvements, and the Government having directed a sum arising from the sale of Crown Lands to be appropriated to similar purposes, it may be confidently assumed, that in a few years, there will be sufficient buildings of every description erected.

By the Act 6th Geo. IV. c. 88, amended by the 7th Geo. IV. c. 4. His Majesty has graciously erected the West India Islands into two Sees, the salaries of the Bishops payable out of the $4\frac{1}{2}$ per cent. duties are four thousand pounds sterling each, with a provision for a retiring pension of one thousand pounds after a service of ten years; and the sum of four thousand three hundred pounds, is at the disposal of the Bishop of Barbados, for the maintenance of Ministers, Catechists, and Schoolmasters in the Diocese, with a limitation that no Minister's salary is to exceed three hundred pounds sterling. This is the first instance of such a provision in the West Indies (except in the case of the Judges of the Prize Courts) and cannot be too highly commended. If the Government wishes to be well and faithfully served by persons adequately qualified to execute the trusts reposed in them, they must secure them a remuneration for their advancing years; in most instances the Colonial salaries, barely afford a decent maintenance, and many persons have been obliged to continue in office from necessity, long after they have been enervated by disease, or disqualified from age. Such a system also tends to check any disposition towards the undue acquirement of the emoluments of office, it will be found most beneficial to both parties, and will confer lasting honour on the provident humanity of His Majesty.

These episcopal appointments have already been of great utility, the inferior clergy have been regulated, and a system adopted of conveying general instruction to the negroes by means of catechists and schoolmasters. The residence of the Bishop is in Barbados, from whence he makes occasional visitations to the different Islands in his Diocese, and it is but justice to add, that the present Bishop is singularly active, and energetic in the performance of his duties towards the untutored race under his spiritual guidance.

The want of education has been a sore evil Education. in the Colonies, but a decided improvement has taken place, under the auspices of the Bishop, and in a few years the parochial schools will manifest their utility. There is a laudable institution by a few coloured persons in Kingstown, for the education of the coloured poor, which with very limited means, has been productive of great advantages, and deserves more patronage and support, than it has hitherto received from the white population. The Le-

SECT. 9. gislature has removed the disabilities attendant on colour, but these concessions will be of no actual benefit to that race, unless they become qualified by education and morals, to assume their advanced station in society, and to perform the duties required of them, and this will depend on their own exertions, to obtain property by their industry, and respect by their integrity; the road to fame and eminence is open to all.

Colonial deficiencies. Notwithstanding all these advantages, there is one lamentable deficiency, which is here stated in the hope of promoting a serious consideration of the subject. There is no public or private establishment for the relief of the aged or sick poor white and free inhabitants, nor even an hospital for casual accidents, while the slaves on estates in their old age are enjoying the comforts of a decent maintenance from the support of their masters; the infirm, or sick white, or free person, has no resource but individual support and charity, and this in a country, where so few ties of relationship exist, must necessarily be precarious.

The leprosy, from a strange and unaccountable neglect, has been gradually increasing, and unless some speedy steps are taken for checking this loathsome infection, it will assume a more determined form, and become an evil of such a magnitude, as to rouse the selfish apathy, which the planters at present indulge in, by whose preponderance in the Legislature, the adoption of those salutary measures, which have frequently been proposed, is prevented. True it is, the pressure of the times is severe, the future prospects are gloomy, the days of West Indian prosperity are probably terminated, but none of these are justifiable reasons why a loathsome and horrid disease should be allowed to establish itself in our posterity, when at a moderate expence, some mode for prevention of the infection at least may be adopted.

SECTION X.

The Grenadines.

THERE is a long chain of small Islands extending in a south westerly direction between Saint
Vincent and Grenada, called by the general
name of the Grenadines. Of these such as
lie to the northward of Carriacou, are compre-
hended within the Government of Saint Vincent.
Since the abandonment of the cultivation of
cotton, the interest and importance of these
Islands has proportionately decreased, and the
account of them will be nearly a barren enu-
meration of names. Their general characteristic is a great fertility of soil, even with the
small quantity of rain, that at present falls
among them, a failure which is to be attributed
to the destruction of the wood, especially the
white cedar, which was abundantly cherished
as a protection to the cotton plantations ;* the

* Close to the sea shore in many of the Islands, the celebrated Manchenille Tree, the Upas of the West Indies,
grows in beautiful luxuriance, even in the salt water. It is
of a splendid green foliage, and bears a fruit not unlike a

pureness and salubrity of the air is very remarkable, the health and longevity of the inhabitants is proportionate, and horned cattle
and sheep, which are reared there, are of excellent quality; but in dry seasons great in-
conveniences are experienced from the want
of water, there are no rivers, the few ponds
are soon dried up, and the tanks or reservoirs
of rain water, which are a necessary appendage
to every establishment, are occasionally exhausted, and great mortality among the stock
is the consequence.

The principal Island is Bequia, containing
three thousand seven hundred acres, in which
are comprised nine sugar estates, cultivated by
about one thousand two hundred and seventy-
three slaves. The principal bay called Admiralty Bay, is very beautiful and commodious,

golden pippin; but it is a most destructive poison, the sap,
which is abundant, if it comes in contact with the skin, will
cause a grievous sore, and even the shade is avoided by
animals, crabs only will eat the leaves, and they become
poisonous in consequence. The quaint old Author Père du
Tertre gives an interesting Account of this and other Trees,
in his " Histoire générale des Antilles," Vol. II. p. 191, Ed.
1667, which deserves to be the basis of any Botanical Work
on these Colonies, that may be undertaken.

sᴇᴄᴛ. 10. where large vessels may be hove down, and repaired with perfect safety, and was destined to
have been a naval station, but the want of
water, was found to be an insuperable objection; at the bottom of the bay is a small town,
with a very neat Church, recently erected. The
Rector whose parish comprehends all the Grenadines, resides here.

In the year 1797, Mr. Charles Warner, a
proprietor in the Island, was inhumanely murdered by two of his own slaves, who were convicted and executed for the crime.

Mustique contains one thousand two hundred
and three acres, and is divided between two
sugar proprietors, the soil is peculiarly fertile,
and the pastures are excellent. There are no
sugar estates in any of the remaining Islands.
Canouan contains one thousand seven hundred
and seventy-seven acres, and is reduced to one
cotton settlement; there is a remarkable reef
of basaltic rocks on the east side of the Island,
which forms a carenage, about twelve feet deep,
on the land side, and on the outer side of the
wall, if it may be so termed, which is perpendicular, and the depth is unfathomable. In the
elevated mountain adjoining, called the Marquis

de Cazeau's Hill, strong indications of iron ore ^{sect. 10.} are visible, and in the clay formation in the vallies, hexagonal crystals, are sometimes found. The Union Island contains two thousand one hundred and fifty acres, and is cultivated in cotton by one proprietor, it is very healthy, and the increase of the slaves is very great; this is the case in most of these Islands, which may be attributed to the light work on cotton estates, the abundance of fish which they obtain with little trouble, and a compulsory sobriety, from the increased difficulty of obtaining rum.

Balliceaux and Battawia are used as Stock Islands; Islet à Quatre is an appendage to Paget Farm Estate in Bequia. Petit Saint Vincent and Myera, each produce a small quantity of cotton; in the latter Island is a very large unfinished mansion of Bath stone, which was fashioned in England, and then sent out to be erected, a conspicuous instance of useless expence, which was afterwards, in 1813, imitated by the Colony of Trinidad, when they proposed to erect a Church, which on importation proved unsuitable, and when half erected, was pulled down.

The remaining Islands of the Group, are either

SECT. 10. used for the purpose of feeding a few sheep, or are barren, and in many cases, almost inaccessible rocks; they all afford coral, which makes excellent lime, and numbers of turtle are taken both by nets and on the shore; conchs and other shell-fish also abound, and the adjoining banks supply an abundance of fish of different descriptions. In the months of February and March, many whales make their appearance in these seas, and some American Vessels occasionally come in quest of them.

The names of the remaining small Islands are as follow :—

Isle of Wash, Church Island, Petit Nevis, Three Ramiers, Pillories, Savan, Petit Bermuda, Petit Canouan, Barbaroux Island, or Petit Curaçoa, Two Taffia Quays, Two Baleines, Two Catholics, Prune Island, Four Tobago Quays, Umbrella Quay and Petit Martinique.

APPENDIX.

No. I.

General State and Disposition of Lands in Saint Vincent, as described by Mr. Byers, in his Survey made January, 1777.

	Acres.
Sold at Public Sale by the Commissioners, leased, and appropriated for public uses -	20,392
Granted to friendly Caribs - -	1,210
Granted to Lieutenant General Monckton -	4,000
Granted to the Caribs by Treaty in 1773 -	27,628
Cultivable Lands undisposed of - -	9,977
Impracticable Land - - - - -	21,079
Total -	84,286

By the General Produce Returns, the Lands forming Estates, are as follow.

	Acres.
Charlotte Parish - - - - -	11,849
Saint George's - - - - -	9,337
Saint Andrew's - - - - -	4,096
Saint David's - - - - -	4,198
Saint Patrick's - - - - -	5,426
Total -	34,906

No. II.

Meteorological Table.

Monthly Mean.	1824.	1825.	1826.	1827.	1828.	1829.
January	79.41	80.17	81.70	80.21	79.09	79.27
February	79.29	79.98	78.90	79.56	78.49	79.42
March -	79.37	81.37	77.52	80.35	79.41	80.32
April -	81.63	82.46	80.08	81.49	80.63	81.28
May -	81.14	83.12	82.02	82.10	82.34	82.63
June -	81.73	82.80	81.78	82.30	82.42	81.86
July -	81.95	83.18	81.86	82.05	82.12	82.12
August -	82.44	83.82	82.37	81.93	83.60	82.71
September	83.53	83.56	82.81	83.02	83.45	83.66
October -	82.08	83.02	82.56	82.02	83.28	83 26
November	81.43	82.11	82.10	82.45	82.79	81.93
December	79.23	80.95	81.55	80.50	80.13	80.03
Year - -	81.10	82.21	81.27	81.50	81.48	81.54

No. III.

Pluviameter.

	1824.	1825.	1826.	1827.	1828.	1829.
January	3.81	3.18	6.06	4.11	4.18	3.16
February	3.04	2.16	7.26	3.70	3.23	2.63
March -	3.64	3.87	4.0	4.51	1.38	1.18
April -	2.72	2.80	1.51	1.39	4.08	1.43
May -	10.07	5.63	3.08	2.88	4.67	4.89
June -	10.19	10.13	10.81	10.61	9.55	9.75
July -	8.95	5.35	7.54	15.89	7.97	7.97
August -	9.69	5.81	8.35	14.14	6.96	8.05
September	6.24	9.61	8.96	5.71	12.02	3.40
October	11.95	8.67	7.33	11.20	10.24	8.15
November	6.58	11.82	6.47	8.36	7.88	7.03
December	5.58	9.90	5.13	5.91	5.54	7.51
Year - -	82.50	78.94	76.52	88.41	77.70	65.15

No. IV.

Population of Saint Vincent and its Dependencies.

Year.	Negroes.	Caribs.	Whites.	Coloured.	Slaves.
1735	6,000	4,000	—	—	—
1764	—	—	2,104	—	7,414
1787	—	—	1,450	300	11,853
1805	—	—	1,600	450	16,500
1812	—	—	1,053	1,482	24,920
1825	—	—	1,301	2,824	—

No. IV. *continued.*

Slave Population of the several Islands, taken from the Triennial Returns in 1820.

Jamaica - - ..	341,812
Barbadoes - - -	78,345
Antigua - - -	31,053
Grenada - .. -	25,677
Saint Vincent . -	24,282
Trinidad - -	23,537
Saint Christopher -	19,817
Dominica - -	16,554
Tobago - -	14,581
Saint Lucia - - -	13,050
Nevis - - -	9,261
Montserrat - -	6,505
Virgin Islands - -	6,000

No. V.

A General Return of the Plantation Slaves, and the Produce raised in Saint Vincent and its Dependencies, from 1820 to 1829.

Year.	Number of Slaves.	Hhds. of Sugar of 15 Cwt.	Punchs. Rum of 110 Gals.	Punchs. Molas. of 100 Gals.	lbs. of Coffee.	lbs. of Cocoa.	Bales of Cotton.
1820	20,582	16,631	8,873	2,123	7,947	11,769	256
1821	20,362	18,331	9,797	2,231	10,620	13,285	402
1822	20,380	19,596	9,630	4,275	7,857	14,653	661
1823	20,077	17,534	4,778	8,118	9,553	9,120	644
1824	20,135	18,549	5,321	7,572	13,743	23,110	628
1825	20,025	20,271	5,674	8,712	8,707	19,269	416
1826	19,889	19,591	5,656	6,461	6,990	26,173	533
1827	19,833	18,340	6,205	5,570	10,103	13,201	251
1828	19,863	21,160	6,627	7,090	1,873	18,434	369
1829	19,603	18,676	6,542	3,973	2,572	12,216	237

No. VI.

A Table of the several Estates, with the Names of the Owners, the Amount of the Produce made during the Years 1827, 1828, and 1829, and the Increase and Decrease of Negroes.

CHARLOTTE PARISH.

Name.	Proprietors.	Acres.	Negroes.	lbs. Sugar.	Galls. Rum.	Galls. Molasses.
Adelphi - -	Devisees of Charles Grant, Jun. ½: John Birch and Ann Montgomery his Wife ¼: Sarah Grant ⅛: and Geo. Colquhoun Grant, Esq. ⅛.	666	511	611,200	17,998	11,300
		:	503	801,600	17,250	16,500
		:	500	630,400	20,136	6,653
New Adelphi	Warner Ottley, Esq. - - -	642	192	420,000	9,290	9,907
		:	192	411,250	5,243	12,180
		:	183	389,300	6,260	9,907
Bellevue - -	Devisees of John Gerard, Esq. -	205	139	330,711	9,660	4,180
		:	134	304,162	9,430	1,980
		235	171	278,413	12,036	....
Colonarie Vale	Walter Coningham, Esq. - -	407	309	532,000	9,300	14,000
		:	310	541,000	10,350	13,650
		:	313	434,000	8,825	7,700

No. VI. CHARLOTTE PARISH *continued.*

Name.	Proprietors.	Acres.	Negroes.	lbs. Sugar.	Galls. Rum.	Galls. Molasses.
Cummacrabou	Ellen and Maria Cruikshank -	200	19	51,700	440	1,890
		:	18	39,100	478	1,308
		:	19	42,550	420	1,200
Dumbarton -	W. M'Gowne and the Heirs of John Johnson - - -	224	66	85,000	1,150	1,500
		:	66	128,400	2,200	1,500
		:	70	120,570	1,540	2,000
Grand Sable -	Devisees of Thomas Browne, Esq. deceased	1,600	657	678,488	18,872	6,820
		:	661	650,717	11,297	14,595
		:	674	525,390	21,850	2,640
Jambou Vale -	Devisees of E. Fleming Akers -	300	134	180,700	2,750	6,700
		:	136	239,000	4,290	7,900
Langley Park -	John Cruikshank, Esq. - -	600	132	225,600	2,200	7,500
		:	300	614,926	16,600	5,052
		:	300	556,053	13,096	4,500
Lot, No. 14. -	Alexander Cumming, Esq. - -	600	294	604,460	20,746	....
		:	334	899,689	16,210	12,273
		:	344	655,565	15,963	14,465
		:	343	649,361	22,608	6,169

No. VI.　CHARLOTTE PARISH *continued.*

Name.	Proprietors.	Acres.	Negroes.	lbs. Sugar.	Galls. Rum.	Galls. Molasses.
Mount Bentinck	Devisees of John and Robert Dalzell	750	293	357,000	6,785	6,600
		..	286	516,000	8,510	10,200
		..	287	564,000	5,981	12,029
Mount Grennan	Devisees of Robert Glasgow deceased	367	273	525,700	12,650	7,200
		..	274	494,200	13,750	5,700
		..	273	436,800	17,500	4,000
Mount William	Heirs of Valentine and Malachi O'Connor	460	220	319,588	10,779	2,318
		..	212	462,762¾	13,260	5,056
		..	197	325,500	13,896	..
New Prospect	James Symon, Esq. - - -	240	160	226,300	3,300	7,600
		..	162	257,950	3,410	9,600
		..	156	274,600	6,160	4,500
Orange Hill -	James Sutherland, Geo. Mackay Sutherland, Ewen Baillie Sutherland, ⅔; and the Devisees of Thomas Patterson, ⅓.	400	286	603,736	16,395	16,687
		..	279	767,244	14,950	25,300
		..	275	668,161	20,702	11,885
Park Hill -	Allan Macdowall, Esq. - - -	350	240	449,680	22,278	..
		..	236	416,820	22,497	..
		..	235	499,860	22,117	..

No. VI. CHARLOTTE PARISH *continued.*

Names.	Proprietors.	Acres.	Negroes.	lbs. Sugar.	Galls. Rum.	Galls. Molasses.
Peruvian Vale	Devisees of George Whitfield deceased	633	326	550,900	9,894	14,077
		..	326	622,500	14,185	15,010
		..	313	517,500	13,068	6,809
Rabacca -	Alexander Cumming, Esq. - -	410	274	748,815	17,921	18,130
		..	280	764,770	19,068	17,459
		..	278	721,626	22,347	5,834
Richland Park	Messrs. Penny and Ames - -	350	97	116,100	3,246	....
		..	96	122,850	3,276	215
		..	94	91,800	1,630	758
Sans Souci -	Devisees of Rob. Glasgow ½; and Alex. McBarnet, Esq. ½ - -	297	249	545,000	14,740	12,400
		..	252	573,184	15,400	13,000
		..	248	459,457	15,400	6,000
Spring - -	Rich. Nichol, Esq. ½; and the Devisees of John Nichol deceased ½. -	300	164	308,000	10,000	....
		..	165	369,000	16,000	....
		..	164	343,300	14,800	....
Three Rivers	Harry Hackshaw, Esq. - -	700	218	340,700	7,906	8,900
		..	216	312,400	7,810	6,500
		..	219	310,700	10,230	2,000

No. VI. CHARLOTTE PARISH *continued.*

Names.	Proprietors.	Acres.	Negroes.	lbs. Sugar.	Galls. Rum.	Galls. Molasses.
Turama	Sir Alexander M'Kenzie, Bart.	600	420	816,859	26,188	18,775
		..	417	940,661	24,100	15,200
		..	406	806,964	24,554	14,775
Union	John Roche Dusent, Esq.	818	593	947,777	26,391	18,995
		..	586	1062,400	41,170	7,000
		..	563	780,800	39,960	....
Waterloo	James Sutherland, Geo. Mackay Sutherland, Ewen Baillie Sutherland, Esqrs.	410	314	630,850	13,402	12,462
		..	314	662,897	15,018	13,529
		..	300	615,991	15,624	11,149
Fancy	Sir William John Struth	..	156	64,400	....	3,252

SAINT GEORGE'S PARISH.

Names.	Proprietors.	Acres.	Negroes.	lbs. Sugar.	Galls. Rum.	Galls. Molasses.
Aker's Narriaqua	Devisees of Edward Fleming Akers	..	87	123,900	880	3,700
		119	88	134,400	660	4,000
		..	86	139,200	110	4,500

No. VI. SAINT GEORGE'S PARISH *continued.*

Names.	Proprietors.	Acres.	Negroes.	lbs. Sugar.	Galls. Rum.	Galls. Molasses.
Argyle	Prince Polignac ⅓; Archibald Macdonald, Esq. ⅓	365	269	442,500	11,000	10,000
		::	267	601,500	11,880	17,000
		::	267	526,500	15,070	11,300
Arno's Vale	Samuel Greatheed, Esq.	449	309	579,750	16,911	7,054
		::	307	682,100	15,490	11,619
		::	297	564,800	13,225	7,320
Bellair	Francis Brown Douglas, Esq.	401	150	215,200	5,720	3,400
		::	150	214,400	6,380	2,500
		::	149	262,701	7,456	2,399
Belmont	John Pemberton Ross, Esq.	256	128	107,200	1,908	2,251
		::	131	125,600	1,455	3,968
		::	129	123,200	2,617	1,177
Belvidere	Thomas Hagart and Elizabeth his Wife	269	194	420,000	10,529	9,725
		::	193	489,000	10,010	10,400
		::	185	421,750	8,030	5,400
Brighton	Gilbert Munro, Esq.	400	169	290,000	8,160	3,862
		::	165	354,000	11,326	5,779
		::	164	253,700	7,973	2,332

No. VI. SAINT GEORGE'S PARISH *continued.*

Names.	Proprietors.	Acres.	Negroes.	lbs. Sugar.	Galls. Rum.	Galls. Molasses.
Calder	Prince Polignac and Archibald Macdonald, Esq.	350	277	427,500	11,270	7,400
		..	273	481,500	10,340	9,600
		..	275	400,500	11,440	6,000
Calder Ridge	Prince Polignac and Archibald Macdonald, Esq.	194	77	148,500	3,080	8,700
		..	78	144,000	1,210	5,300
		..	77	129,000	770	3,000
Cane Garden	Samuel Gregg, Esq.	..	92	117,240	1,056	4,105
		82	92	136,500	1,017	4,472
		..	89	107,732	1,998	1,488
Cane Hall	William Winn, Esq.	392	153	194,200	9,150	....
		..	196	200,300	10,538	....
		..	187	281,000	12,564	5,864
Carapan	Archibald and William Alves, Esqrs.	240	163	312,180	7,764	6,131
		..	165	361,600	8,090	3,663
		..	159	288,200	8,028	6,157
Coubamarou	Devisees of John Dalzell deceased	181	199	215,250	5,574	11,119
		..	190	308,800	4,415	3,549
		..	180	249,000	10,844	

No. VI. SAINT GEORGE'S PARISH *continued.*

Names.	Proprietors.	Acres.	Negroes.	lbs. Sugar.	Galls. Rum.	Galls. Molasses.
Diamond, Lower	Jonathan Morgan, Esq.	199	191	319,500	11,684	2,633
		..	192	366,000	11,198	5,377
		..	192	322,500	10,097	2,399
Diamond, Upper	Lady Bolton	189	124	217,500	8,166	2,441
		..	123	340,256	6,701	7,221
		..	114	225,736	7,272	1,997
		193	188	295,500	8,142	4,221
Escape	Jonathan Morgan, Esq.	..	185	354,000	7,904	5,522
		..	182	323,100	6,554	5,373
		202	149	155,908	2,090	2,700
Evesham Vale	James Huggins Lacroix, Esq.	..	152	190,400	2,860	3,700
		..	149	201,600	3,872	5,000
		420	246	360,192	8,724	5,130
Fairhall	James Adam Gordon, Esq.	..	245	281,176	4,810	7,457
		..	238	321,210	8,048	4,709
		300	127	207,890	3,500	2,940
Fountain	Rene Augier, Henry Lindow Lindow, Esqrs.	..	129	278,616	2,875	7,000
		..	129	212,299	2,070	5,405

No. VI. SAINT GEORGE'S PARISH *continued.*

Names.	Proprietors.	Acres.	Negroes.	lbs. Sugar.	Galls. Rum.	Galls. Molasses.
Golden Vale -	James Lacroix, Esq.	260	76	112,000	2,310	500
		..	76	71,050	1,100	1,900
		..	75	75,400	1,045	2,000
Harmony Hall	Thomas Choppin, Esq.	147	93	109,500	2,596	1,305
		..	92	159,600	5,564	1,802
		..	92	127,500	1,505	1,700
Kingstown Park	Rev. Charles Paul	142	131	103,500	349	2,900
		..	133	141,000	463	4,950
		..	132	96,000	1,995	1,868
Strowan Cottage	Richard Robertson, Esq.	270	66	85,000	220	3,177
		..	67	80,600	992	2,750
		..	68	95,100	1,049	2,823
Liberty Lodge	John Small, Esq.	200	47	60,000	1,100	1,400
		..	49	96,000	1,216	3,255
		..	48	41,000	812	805
Mount Pleasant	Mrs. Douglas	306	249	480,400	11,026	10,667
		..	250	517,600	12,702	8,984
		..	245	488,800	13,000	6,412

No. VI. SAINT GEORGE'S PARISH *continued.*

Names.	Proprietors.	Acres.	Negroes.	lbs. Sugar.	Galls. Rum.	Galls. Molasses.
Prospect	Sir William John Struth	464	333	536,000	14,225	7,716
		..	334	443,858	14,512	8,498
		..	331	364,000	11,499	5,484
Ratho Mill	Richard Rees, Esq.	342	275	279,400	8,400	7,550
		..	279	335,500	10,400	8,366
		..	276	265,200	10,600	2,380
Redemption	George Sharpe, Esq.	600	126	133,500	3,933	2,577
		..	130	136,500	3,897	2,452
		..	127	238,650	3,520	7,200
Revolution Hall	Wm. Glenn Ponsonby, John Ponsonby, George Ponsonby, and Taylor Hammond Ponsonby, Esqrs.	186	103	154,400	4,756	2,512
		..	102	174,000	5,448	3,274
		..	102	124,503	4,255	1,824
Richmond Hill	Charles James French, Esq.	280	176	230,500	3,191	9,392
		..	178	297,000	4,950	10,000
		..	175	238,650	3,520	7,200
Rivulet	Duncan Brown and Duncan Forbes Sutherland, Esqrs.	230	90	99,750	8,484	860
		..	93	168,000	3,806	2,530
		..	100	99,000	1,840	2,090

No. VI. SAINT GEORGE'S PARISH *continued.*

Names.	Proprietors.	Acres.	Negroes.	lbs. Sugar.	Galls. Rum.	Galls. Molasses.
Sion Hill - -	Hon. W. Fraser, W. M. Alexander, Claud Neilson, and Boyd Alexander, Esqrs.	340	139	240,000	2,772	8,480
		..	138	300,000	4,800	9,507
		..	133	240,000	4,786	5,942
Villa - -	Devisees of John Robley and Charles Brooke, Esqrs. - - -	339	137	289,000	7,900	5,530
		..	136	333,500	9,700	4,800
		..	133	291,500	10,227	1,223

SAINT ANDREW'S PARISH.

Names.	Proprietors.	Acres.	Negroes.	lbs. Sugar.	Galls. Rum.	Galls. Molasses.
Camden Par	Charles Phillips, Esq. - -	330	165	292,000	7,900	7,600
		..	164	350,000	8,655	7,884
		..	163	315,000	12,108	5,223
Cane Grove -	James Wilson, Esq. - -	598	231	500,000	6,000	22,319
		..	223	640,000	7,055	28,457
		..	223	538,525	6,017	22,336

No. VI. SAINT ANDREW'S PARISH *continued.*

Names.	Proprietors.	Acres.	Negroes.	lbs. Sugar.	Galls. Rum.	Galls. Molasses.
Cane Wood -	Devisees of John Dalzell deceased -	541	195	224,000	3,910	8,315
		..	196	274,500	2,981	10,902
		..	198	256,000	6,259	9,011
Clare Valley -	John Snell, Esq. -	443	131	236,500	1,940	12,013
		..	130	280,000	3,700	13,145
		..	129	260,800	2,331	11,332
Hope -	John Inglet Fortescue, Esq. •	216	81	112,500	1,700	3,200
		..	82	121,500	2,657	3,228
		..	82	100,500	1,892	1,718
L'Ance Joyeuse	Devisees of John B. Questel, Esq. -	190	90	107,250	348	4,213
		..	88	139,500	197	5,136
		..	88	120,000	4,478	1,938
Montrose -	Devisees of Andrew Rose, Esq. -	430	113	173,200	1,650	5,100
		..	115	201,000	2,860	6,400
		..	117	177,600	967	6,545
Ottley Hall -	William Boyd, Esq. -	200	100	154,240	3,105	4,300
		..	92	175,500	4,310	5,920
		..	87	129,690	3,509	1,975

No. VI. SAINT ANDREW'S PARISH *continued.*

Names.	Proprietors.	Acres.	Negroes.	lbs. Sugar.	Galls. Rum.	Galls. Molasses.
Pembroke	Devisees of John Robley and Charles Brooke, Esq.	453	198	331,800	13,195	2,679
		..	193	433,500	16,377	4,132
		..	194	391,000	15,119	1,200
Pennistons	Jonathan Morgan and —— Jennings, Esqrs.	250	116	180,341	3,520	3,360
		..	115	205,500	4,180	3,780
		..	117	189,000	6,019	1,155
Queensbury	Leonard Slater, Esq.	415	153	244,500	4,779	8,020
		..	152	285,000	4,406	10,285
		..	149	237,250	6,312	3,873
Retreat	Devisees of Edward Jackson deceased, and Charles Kirby, Esq.	..	30	51,400	....	3,164
		..	30	61,600	....	3,909
		..	30	68,600	....	3,099

SAINT PATRICK'S PARISH.

Names.	Proprietors.	Acres.	Negroes.	lbs. Sugar.	Galls. Rum.	Galls. Molasses.
Aker's Layou	Edmund Fleming Akers, Esq.	250	37	36,670	180	1,544
		..	46	62,900	228	2,200
		..	53	51,476	345	2,235

No. VI. SAINT PATRICK'S PARISH *continued.*

Names.	Proprietors.	Acres.	Negroes.	lbs. Sugar.	Galls. Rum.	Galls. Molasses.
Belle Isle	John Greathead, Esq.	486	133	141,400	3,850	1,000
		..	131	120,000	1,200	3,723
		..	129	117,000	1,496	1,870
Cumberland	Richard Rees, Esq.	245	120	139,500	4,945	1,425
		..	117	180,000	4,830	2,660
		..	109	168,000	6,353	1,752
Grove	Trustees of Mrs. Hill	315	94	67,800	1,906	1,167
		..	89	67,720	1,756	1,349
		..	84	65,000	1,994	459
Kearton's	Mary Kearton and Henry Lindow Lindow, Esq.	384	124	164,400	1,608	7,619
		..	120	184,500	1,930	8,216
		..	120	177,000	3,226	4,765
L'Ance Mahaut	Thomas Wilkinson, Esq.	176	54	67,700	....	3,100
		..	53	78,000	....	4,200
		..	58	78,800	....	4,100
Mount Hope	Macduff Fyfe, Esq.	173	54	54,000	475	2,600
		..	53	75,000	300	2,000
		..	59	67,500	465	2,995

No. VI. SAINT PATRICK'S PARISH *continued*.

Names.	Proprietors,	Acres,	Negroes,	lbs. Sugar,	Galls. Rum,	Galls. Molasses.
Mount Wynne	Richard Nichol, and Devisees of John Nichol, Esq. - - - -	500	225	292,600	12,555	....
		..	223	349,600	17,042	112
		..	220	298,000	13,992	....
Palmisle Park	Devisees of Edward Jackson, Esq.	200	131	76,200	827	3,030
		..	132	113,172	1,263	4,303
		..	122	115,280	2,269	3,094
Peter's Hope	Devisees of William Gurley, Esq.	400	105	138,500	3,980	....
		..	101	195,000	7,200	....
		..	101	157,500	5,290	....
Reversion -	Devisees of Thomas Morgan deceased	250	96	85,440	1,028	2,868
		..	94	137,070	1,770	5,257
		..	90	150,116	1,815	6,125
Rutland Vale	Devisees of Josias Jackson, Esq. -	600	263	342,000	9,707	10,610
		..	256	546,328	8,000	16,500
		..	249	438,200	5,940	17,200
Spring -	Gordon Augustus Thomson, Esq.	684	91	51,800	1,479	660
		..	98	57,000	1,140	
		..	82	70,000	1,210	1,400

No. VI. SAINT PATRICK'S PARISH *continued.*

Names.	Proprietors.	Acres.	Negroes.	lbs. Sugar.	Galls. Rum.	Galls. Molasses.
Wallilabo -	Alexander McBarnet, Esq.	500	247	180,000	5,060	3,000
		..	198	281,636	3,670	7,502
		..	190	257,796	5,369	1,361
Westwood -	Dr. Coull -	265	107	99,000	3,506	1,828
		..	106	119,000	3,610	3,743
		..	101	110,060	4,648	1,245

SAINT DAVID'S PARISH.

Names.	Proprietors.	Acres.	Negroes.	lbs. Sugar.	Galls. Rum.	Galls. Molasses.
Belmont -	Alexander Cruikshank, Esq. -	240	77	141,100	914	2,990
		..	76	138,000	1,167	4,000
		..	74	97,500	1,265	2,310
Bostock Park	John and Nathaniel Bassnett Cropper and John Bolton, Esqrs. -	900	184	219,900	3,933	4,209
		..	180	253,500	5,334	4,197
		..	181	241,500	4,386	3,421

No. VI. SAINT DAVID'S PARISH *continued.*

Names.	Proprietors.	Acres.	Negroes.	lbs. Sugar.	Galls. Rum.	Galls. Molasses.
Heirs of T. Fraser	Thomas Fraser	214	59	6,974	..	....
		..	..	Coffee and Cocoa.	..	....
Golden Grove	Christopher Punnett, Esq.	350	134	178,500	2,645	4,950
		..	130	196,500	3,220	6,600
		..	126	202,500	2,415	8,500
Millingtons -	Thomas Crookenden, Esq.	108	113	112,500	6,398	....
		..	114	139,200	7,695	....
		..	115	128,000	5,924	....
Mount Alexander	Devisees of J. D. Questel, Esq.	300	111	97,500	2,970	....
		..	104	34,500	230	344
		..	102	36,000	935	....
Petit Bordel and Sharpe's	Michael White, Esq.	320	188	286,500	9,130	3,500
		..	187	297,600	16,390	1,500
		..	186	273,000	5,720	700
Richmond -	Patrick Cruikshank, Esq.	500	356	682,438	20,123	6,241
		..	355	755,695	16,048	3,061
		..	347	723,167	18,142	8,238

No. VI. SAINT DAVID'S PARISH *continued.*

Names.	Proprietors.	Acres.	Negroes.	lbs. Sugar.	Galls. Rum.	Galls. Molasses.
Richmond Vale, or Fitzhugh's	Thomas Fitzhugh, Esq. - -	388	133 133 125	207,000 207,000 186,000	4,633 3,826 4,481	3,684 5,079 1,642
Rose Bank -	Devisees of George Dalzell and of Joseph W. Mayer deceased	250	167 167 165	223,300 269,000 251,000	1,276 1,320 1,150	7,400 9,000 9,400
Wallibo - -	Devisees of John Grant and of Lewis Grant deceased - -	500	217 213 206	256,000 331,500 331,500	5,601 4,800 6,467	5,078 8,600 7,436

ISLAND OF BEQUIA.

Names.	Proprietors.	Acres.	Negroes.	lbs. Sugar.	Galls. Rum.	Galls. Molasses.
Belmont -	W. T. Dickenson, Esq. - -	105	142 144 143	25,500 58,500 25,509	770 1,650 770	770 1,980 660

No. VI. ISLAND OF BEQUIA *continued.*

Names.	Proprietors.	Acres.	Negroes.	lbs. Sugar.	Galls. Rum.	Galls. Molasses.
Friendship -	Devisees of Charles John Warner deceased	483	89	78,000	1,887	1,888
		: :	90	123,000	2,854	3,660
		: :	88	48,000	738	1,188
Hope -	Devisees of John Henderson deceased	300	176	36,000	1,900	....
		: :	177	61,600	3,190	....
		: :	177	41,000	2,750	300
Industry -	William T. Dickenson, Esq.	1,000	202	67,500	1,540	1,800
		: :	207	78,400	1,980	2,400
		: :	202	78,000	2,640	2,530
Mount Pleasant	Devisees of Peter Audain and of Mrs. Herries	200	61	39,200	1,035	600
		: :	62	67,200	1,540	2,030
		: :	62	32,068	579	1,040
Paget Farm -	William Stowe, Esq.	220	134	74,000	1,380	2,300
		: :	140	116,000	1,300	8,200
		: :	140	141,000	1,500	6,400
Reform -	Mons. Marricheau and others.	200	100	33,000	460	880
		: :	105	70,500	1,610	2,200
		: :	104	34,500	880	990

No. VI. ISLAND OF BEQUIA *continued.*

Names.	Proprietors.	Acres.	Negroes.	lbs. Sugar.	Galls. Rum.	Galls. Molasses.
Spring	William Rose Scott, Thomas Scott, and Walter Scott ½; the Devisees of Charles Warner ½.	619	183	156,000	4,504	4,200
		..	184	238,500	6,490	6,800
		..	181	197,202	5,865	5,940
Union	William Rose, Esq.	206	156	46,600	1,840	1,980
		..	164	93,600	4,235	1,800
		..	160	53,300	2,750	600

ISLAND OF MUSTIQUE.

Names.	Proprietors.	Acres.	Negroes.	lbs. Sugar.	Galls. Rum.	Galls. Molasses.
Cheltenham	Christopher Punnett, Esq.	663	222	204,000	5,280	7,700
		..	229	313,500	6,600	19,000
		..	231	181,000	3,520	7,360
Adelphi	Messrs. Triminghams	1,992	134	73,500	410	7,163
		..	188	90,900	6,500	5,000
		..	139	87,000	1,320	5,000

No. VI. *continued.* ISLAND OF CANOUAN.

Name.	Proprietor.	Acres.	Negroes.	lbs. Cotton.
Carenage -	Mrs. Snagg - - -	600	214	27,000
		..	236	36,000
		..	235	29,700

UNION ISLAND.

Name.	Proprietors.	Acres.	Negroes.	lbs. Cotton.
Union Island	Devisees of Samuel Span - -	2,057	391	43,861
		..	396	50,757
		..	400	50,948

No. VII.

Average Prices of Sugars.

Year.	Average Price.		Weight of Cask.	Duty.		Gross.			Charges including Duty			Profits.		
	s.	d.	Cwt.	s.	d.	£.	s.	d.	£.	s.	d.	£.	s.	d.
1791	67	4	13	12	4	43	15	4	13	10	10	30	4	6
1792	69	4	..	....		45	1	4	13	10	10	31	10	6
1793	70	4	..	....		45	14	4	15	16	4	29	18	0
1794	54	0	..	15	0	35	2	0	17	11	0	17	11	0
1795	77	5	..	....		50	2	1	17	17	6	32	4	7
1796	77	0	..	....		50	1	0	17	17	6	32	3	6
1797	81	6	..	17	6	52	19	6	19	16	6	33	3	0
1798	86	0	..	19	4	55	18	0	21	0	4	34	17	8
1799	75	0	..	20	0	48	15	0	21	15	6	26	19	6
1800	74	0	..	....		48	2	0	21	15	6	26	6	6
1801	64	0	..	....		41	12	0	22	2	0	19	10	0
1802	54	0	..	....		35	7	5	22	2	0	13	5	5
1803	67	0	..	24	0	43	11	0	22	2	0	21	9	0
1804	80	0	..	26	6	52	2	0	26	6	6	25	15	6
1805	76	0	.	27	0	49	8	0	26	19	6	22	8	6
1806	68	0	..	....		43	14	0	27	6	0	16	8	0
1807	....		..	....		....			....			....		
1808	....		..	....		....			....			....		
1809	76	0	12½	....		47	3	3	25	9	9	21	13	6
1810	77	6	..	27	0	49	12	6	25	6	0	24	6	6
1811	67	0	..	....		45	5	0	28	2	11	17	2	1
1812	77	0	13	....		50	10	1	26	16	11	23	13	2
1813	92	0	..	....		60	19	2	29	10	10	31	8	4
1814	99	6	..	....		70	12	7	30	15	8	39	16	11
1815	99	0	14½	....		68	15	2	29	17	11	38	17	3
1816	81	0	..	....		58	5	8	27	15	6	30	10	2
1817	81	6	..	....		58	5	6	25	9	6	32	15	0
1818	84	9	..	....		60	1	11	27	1	4	33	0	7
1819	70	0	..	....		50	2	10	26	3	9	23	19	1
1820	67	6	..	....		47	9	11	25	8	11	22	1	0
1821	61	9	..	....		44	8	2	25	15	10	19	2	4
1822	59	6	..	....		43	6	8	25	15	7	17	11	1
1823	61	0	..	....		43	16	3	25	15	6	18	0	9
1824	59	0	..	....		41	17	11	25	0	7	16	17	4
1825	68	0	..	....		49	5	7	25	19	2	23	6	5
1826	....		..	....		....			....			....		
1827	....		..	....		....			....			....		
1828	....		..	....		....			....			....		
1829	53	0	..	27	0	37	17	7	26	3	1	11	14	6

No. VIII.

Estimated Expences of a Sugar Estate, with a Water-mill, (in the Windward quarter) 500 Acres of Land, 300 Slaves, 100 Head of Mules and Horned Cattle, and to make 300 Hogsheads of Sugar, weighing at the King's Beam 15 Cwt. Net, 150 Puncheons of Rum, and 50 Puncheons of Molasses, the value of which is £60,000. Sterling.

ARTICLES PAYABLE IN RUM.		Currency.
40,000 lbs. Cod Fish, at 44s. - -		£. 940
20,000 Red Oak Staves, at £.28 per m̄.	‿	560
25,000 White Pine Boards, at £.16 - -		400
		£. 1,900
150 Puncheons of Rum - £.3,000		
50 Ditto Molasses - - 700		
		3,700
Equal in Cash to £.1420.*		£.1,800

PAYMENTS IN CASH.	
Manager's salary - - -	500
Five other White servants -	850
Medical Attendance - - -	150
Taxes £.420. Town Agent £.150 -	570
Pitch Pine Lumber, Shingles, Cedar Posts, Hard Wood, Flour and Rice at Christmas, and for other small Cash articles - - -	350
	2,420
Less Balance of Rum Crop -	1,420
	£.1.000

* When Rum is taken in payment for the articles which are sold for this species of barter, the estimated price is 3s. Currency per gallon, and 72s. for each Puncheon; but when it is given for Cash articles, or sold for money, the price varies with the demand, from 2s. 9d., 2s. 4½d., to 2s. 3d., and the Puncheons are only taken at 60s. each.

No. VIII. *continued.*

To be added to the Sterling Account at Exchange 245, say - - - - £. 410

Home Invoice for Negro Cloathing, Medicines, Wine, Irish Provisions, Oatmeal, Oil Cake, Saddlery, Hoops, Nails, Hoes, Bills, Coopers, Carpenters, Masons, and Blacksmiths' Tools ; Iron; 100 Puns. Coals; Temper and Building Lime, Bricks and Tiles } 1,000

Mules and Cattle £.100. Droghage £.270 - 370

       * To be charged against Sugar Crop. Sterling £.1,780
       Annual Charges as above - £.1,780
       † Interest on Capital, £.60,000, at
       5 per Cent. per Ann. - - 3,000

                         £.4,780 4,780
By 300 Hhds. Sugar of 15 Cwt. Net at £15. per Hhd. 4,500

                 Deficiency - £. 280

* This is the usual Annual Estimate, but there are occasionally other heavy charges, such as a Mill, a Still, Sugar Pans, &c. &c.

† See Humboldt's Personal Narrative, VII. 179, for an Estimate of the Expences of a Sugar Estate in Cuba, by which it appears, that an invested Capital of 470,000 piastres will not give a return of more than 60,500 piastres for the year 1825, being rather more than 6 per cent., but at the present prices, not 4 per cent. would be realised.

No. IX.

Account Sales of 17 Casks of Sugar in 1809.

	£.	s.	d.
To Customs on 208 cwt. 3 qrs. at 27s., fees 12s. 6d. }	282	8	9
Dock dues on ditto at 9d. per cwt.	7	16	7
Samples - - - -	0	8	6
Freight 9s. per cwt. Primage 17d.	95	2	10
Interest on the above - -	2	17	0
Stamps - - - -	0	7	6
Insurance from fire 5 per cent.	1	16	0
Brokerage ½ per cent. (on Gross sales)	3	11	10
Commission 2½ per cent. (on ditto)	17	19	8
Charges -	412	8	8
Net proceeds to the Planter's credit	307	0	1
	£719	8	9

	cwt. qrs. lbs.	£.	s..	d.
By 17 Casks weighing	230 1 17			
Tare - -	24 3 11			
Net - - 205 2 6 } at 70s. per cwt. }		719	8	9
		£719	8	9

No. IX. continued.

Account Sales of 28 Casks of Sugar in 1829.

	£.	s.	d.		£.	s.	d.
Insurance on £.560 at 25s. 7 0 0 Com., Policy, and Stamps, 4 7 6 }	11	7	6	By 28 Casks weighing Net 403 1 20 at 55s. *(cwt. qrs. lbs.)*	1,109	8	6
Duty on 414 cwt. 25lbs. at 27s. fees 10s.	559	14	0				
Freight at 5s. and Primage and Pierage	104	15	7				
Trade, Cooperage, and Stamps -	3	0	10				
Dock dues - - - -	13	16	2				
Rent - - - -	2	5	2				
Insurance from fire - -	1	15	0				
Interest - - -	7	3	8				
Brokerage ½ per cent. on £.1,109 8s. 6d.	5	10	11				
Commission 2½ per cent. on ditto.	27	14	8				
	737	3	6				
Net proceeds to the Planter's credit	372	5	0				
£.1,109	8	6			1,109	8	6

Note.—It will be seen on the inspection of these accounts how heavy the charges are against the Planter : first, he is charged with the Duties, and Interest upon that outlay, and on the Freight ; the former he is reimbursed by the Purchaser, who has four months' time for payment allowed, within which period if he becomes bankrupt, or any other accident happens, the Planter loses not only his Sugar, but the amount of the Duties. He is next charged Commission and Brokerage on the Gross sales, which are more than double the Net proceeds.

It is reported the Government is about to make some alteration in the mode of collecting the Duties, and that in future they are to be paid by the Purchaser. This will be a great relief, and is no more than strict justice towards the Planter.

No. IX. *continued.*

Account Sales of 20 Puncheons of Rum in 1815.

	£.	s.	d.		£.	s.	d.
To Fees and Excise Bond - -	1	2	0	By 20 Punchs. Rum, 2,212 Galls.			
Dock dues 1d. per Gall. & 1s. per Punch. -	10	4	4	at 2s. 7d. - - - -	288	3	9
Guaging and Cutting at 6d. -	0	10	0	Landing Charges - - - -	5	0	0
Freight 9d. per Gall. Primage 17d. -	84	7	4				
Interest on the above - -	3	11	6				
Rent - - - -	20	3	4				
Advertising Sale, and Stamps -	1	4	0				
Insurance from fire at 5 per cent.	0	14	7				
Brokerage 1 per cent. - -	2	18	7				
Commission 2½ per cent. - -	7	6	7				
Charges, &c. -	132	2	3				
Net proceeds to the Planter's credit	161	1	6				
	£293	3	9		£293	3	9

No. X.

IMPORTS FROM

Years.	Great Britain.			West Indies.			North America.			Foreign States.			Total.		
	£.	s.	d.	£.	s.	d.	£.	s.	d.	£.	s.	d.	£.	s.	d.
1827	89,235	0	0	38,158	6	4	37,758	9	6	22,612	9	5	187,764	3	3
1828	87,137	9	5	17,475	15	8	45,429	16	2	28,092	3	5	178,135	4	8
1829	84,513	8	8	31,161	10	0	41,706	8	6	27,922	0	8	185,303	7	10

EXPORTS TO

Years.	Great Britain.			West Indies.			North America.			Foreign States.			Total.		
	£.	s.	d.	£.	s.	d.	£.	s.	d.	£.	s.	d.	£.	s.	d.
1827	426,529	0	0	28,474	3	6	19,529	10	0	6,804	15	0	481,637	8	6
1828	436,540	18	0	20,170	16	6	126,429	10	0	5,369	3	4	588,510	7	10
1829	433,964	15	0	23,901	12	10	22,389	10	0	1,323	11	0	481,579	8	10

No. XI.

SHIPPING. OUTWARDS TO

Year.	Great Britain.		British Colonies.		Foreign States.		Total.	
	Number of Vessels.	Tons.	Number of Vessels.	Tons.	Number of Vessels.	Tons.		
1827	54	14,238	163	12,291	116	5,605	333	32,134
1828	58	16,906	207	13,037	144	6,243	409	36,186
1829	51	14,081	255	16,726	114	6,821	420	37,628

INWARDS FROM

Year.	Great Britain.		British Colonies.		Foreign States.		Total.	
	Number of Vessels.	Tons.	Number of Vessels.	Tons.	Number of Vessels.	Tons.		
1827	61	16,070	150	12,852	114	5,328	325	34,450
1828	59	15,711	149	16,714	160	8,531	368	40,956
1829	59	16,520	210	15,057	125	6,104	394	37,681

No. XII.

*Military and Naval Expenditure for the West Indies,
exclusive of Jamaica.* 1818.

Sterling.

	£.	s.	d.
Commissary General - - - -	93,603	12	10½
Allowances under General Orders -	28,654	13	4
Quarter and Barrack Department -	109,619	16	6
Hospital Department - - -	4,566	10	8
Army Vessels - - - - -	4,512	13	9
Payments under Warrants - - -	3,389	3	3
Allowances, Commissary's Department -	16,338	16	3
Ordnance - - - - - -	75,030	0	0
Store-keeper General - - -	1,110	17	11
Commisssioners of Accounts - -	3,502	0	0
Naval Yard - - - - -	10,090	0	0
Staff Pay - - - - - -	20,629	6	10¼
Regimental Subsistence - - -	100,091	13	5¼
Naval Expenditure - - - -	200,000	0	0
	£.670,139	4	10

The Saint Vincent average of the above expense is about
£.44,000 ; no doubt the expenses since 1818 have been
gradually decreased, but the returns have not been made
public : the above are taken from one of the Works of that
able and zealous advocate of the West Indies, James
M'Queen, Esq.

No. XIII.

Expenditure of the Island from the Treasurer's Books.

	Currency £.	s.	d.			Currency £.	s.	d.
1806	16,433	2	6	1818	-	37,858	12	3
1807	28,536	8	5	1819	-	85,126	8	6
1808	22,504	0	8	1820	-	39,710	8	10
1809	16,158	1	2	1821	-	18,130	2	3
1810	19,868	18	2	1822	-	37,712	1	2
1811	21,253	12	3	1823	-	29,908	10	4
1812	19,583	18	8	1824	-	38,034	3	5
1813	24,123	19	6	1825	-	23,134	5	8
1814	22,036	5	4	1826	-	26,173	16	7
1815	18,633	0	7	1827	-	32,327	14	4
1816	24,250	8	2	1828	-	31,671	7	11
1817	22,133	11	1	1829	-	25,361	5	2

No. XIV.

Estimated Expenses of the Colony for the Year 1829.

SALARIES TO PUBLIC OFFICERS.

	Currency.		
His Honour the President -	£. 3,333	6	8
Chief Justice - - - -	2,000	0	0
Attorney General - - -	500	0	0
Colonial Secretary, as Clerk of the } Council - - - - - }	200	0	0
Clerk of the Assembly - - -	500	0	0
Messenger & Housekeeper to Assembly	200	0	0
Clerk to the Magistrates - -	50	0	0
Registrar of Slaves - - -	250	0	0
Treasurer - - - - -	1,200	0	0
Colonial Agent, £.320 sterling at 240 } Exchange - - - - }	768	0	0
Signal Men - - - -	85	0	0
Clerk of the Market - - -	100	0	0
Overseer of the Tread-mill - -	150	0	0
Chief Constable - - - -	300	0	0
Three extra Constables - -	300	0	0
	9,936	6	8

MILITARY ESTABLISHMENT.

Adjutant of Southern Regiment of Militia	100	0	0
Ditto of King's Companies - -	50	0	0
Ditto of Queen's Companies - -	50	0	0
Armourer - - - - -	100	0	0
Repairing Military Roads - -	410	0	0
	710	0	0

CLERICAL ESTABLISHMENT.

Estimated Expences of Repairing } Churches £.200, stating Exchange } at 240, is - - - }	480	0	0
Rector of Saint George's and St. } Andrew's Parishes - - }	1,060	0	0
Parish Clerk ditto, ditto	100	0	0
Organist ditto, ditto	300	0	0
Officiating Minister of Charlotte Parish	700	0	0
Parish Clerk of ditto	66	0	0
Rector of Leeward Parishes - -	866	0	0
Ditto of Grenadines - - -	766	0	0
Amount of Tenders for building a Church in Bequia, - - £.4,779 Less paid - 500	4,279	0	0
Parsonage in Charlotte Parish -	2,200	0	0
	10,817	0	0

No. XIV. *continued.*

	£.	s.	d.
Brought forward - -	21,463	6	8

ANNUITIES.

	£.	s.	d.		£.	s.	d.
To Militia Men, &c. - -	286	0	0				
Manumitted Slaves - - -	448	0	0				
Arrears - - - - -	732	0	0		1,466	0	0

PUBLIC ROADS.

	£.	s.	d.		£.	s.	d.
Annual Repairs - - -	2,516	0	0				
Ditto, Vigie and Owia Roads -	199	0	0				
Arrears of Annual Repairs -	2,091	17	0				
Allowed extra for heavy Rains -	500	0	0		5,306	17	0

MISCELLANEOUS.

	£.	s.	d.		£.	s.	d.
House Rent to the Commander in Chief - - - -	666	13	4				
Estimate for special Service -	2,960	0	0				
Building a Government House -	10,000	0	0				
Accounts against the Public -	3,000	0	0				
Arrears of ditto - - -	3,286	7	6				
Due the Church Contractors -	352	4	11				
Allowed for Contingencies - -	3,000	0	0				
Rewards under the Slave Act to Nurses, Midwives, and Mothers for rearing and taking Care of Children - - - -	4,000	0	0		27,265	5	9
					£55,501	9	5

No. XIV. continued. Taxes, &c. required to meet the annexed Estimate.

		£.	s.	d.
28,015,112 lbs. Sugar	at 45s.	630,340	0	0
771,952 Galls. Rum	at 3s.	115,792	16	0
433,531 Galls. Molasses	at 2s.	43,353	2	0
2,572 lbs. Coffee	at 1s.	128	12	0
12,216 lbs. Cocoa	at 1s.	610	16	0
87,709 lbs. Cotton	at 1s.	4,385	9	0
21,250 lbs. Arrow Root	at 1s.	1,062	10	0
Produce		795,673	5	0
Poll Tax		75,000	0	0
House Tax		5,700	0	0

£.876,373 5 0 at 2½ per Cent. £.21,909 6 7

	£.	s.	d.
1,600 Negroes, at 4s.	320	0	0
Due by the Treasurer's Account to 31st. December, 1829	2,675	18	10
Deficiency of White Servants	1,000	0	0
Duties on Liquors	200	0	0
Powder Officer	400	0	0
Transient Traders	100	0	0
Heirs of Robert Paul	1,000	0	0
Duties received by the Custom House	100	0	0
Outstanding Taxes	15,050	10	10

£.42,755 16 3

No. XV.

The Memorial of the Planters and Merchants concerned in the Island of Saint Vincent, to the Duke of Portland, Mr. Pitt, and Mr. Dundas,

Humbly represents,

That at the time of the cession of the Island of Saint Vincent to his Majesty's Government by the Crown of France, by treaty, dated one thousand seven hundred and sixty-three, a part of the Island was occupied by a few Red Indians, and by about two thousand descendants of African negroes, who had escaped from an African slave ship, wrecked on the coast of a neighbouring island, towards the close of the last century.

That it was in contemplation of His Majesty's Government in the first instance to remove off these negroes, and transplant them to the coast of Africa, or some island adjacent.

That in one thousand seven hundred and sixty-eight, in consequence of representations that they might remain at St. Vincent without prejudice to the colony, instructions were sent to the Commissioners to appropriate and regulate their settlement in a Quarter of the island.

That whatever appearances of loyalty or peaceable demeanour had induced the Commissioners to make such representations against their removal, or His Majesty's Ministers to adopt them, the Black Caribs (so improperly though generally termed) quickly shewed a disposition little worthy of the royal favour, or sovereign protection, by withdrawing their allegiance and attacking the King's troops attending the surveyors then marking out the public roads. Such attack was by the Caribs avowed

as a measure determined on by them to prevent His
Majesty's forces having any passage or communication
within the country they chose to occupy, and proceeded
to such extremity, that at great charge and expense, an
army under General Dalrymple was employed to reduce
them, and with views on their being subdued, to enforce
the original purpose of their removal. After several
months of cruel warfare, it was thought expedient to relinquish the idea of removing these Africans, and terms
of compromise were entered into in one thousand seven
hundred and seventy-three, and the chiefs signed conditions and took the oaths of allegiance to His Majesty.
From the very date of taking such oaths, and promising
to be good and faithful subjects, they have omitted
severally, or in the aggregate, no opportunity of treason,
or giving assistance to His Majesty's enemies.

That in the last war they called in the French, and
assisted them in wresting the Island of Saint Vincent
from the sovereignty of Great Britain, but restrained by
the then mild and generous tempers of the French
officers, did not display their natural and ferocious
tempers, the fatal effects of which necessitate the present
application of your Memorialists.

That during the present war, in April, one thousand
seven hundred and ninety-four, His Majesty's Governor
and Council of Saint Vincent, well apprised of the spirit
of perfidy and disloyalty which had ever shewn itself
among the Black Caribs, (or rather negro invaders and
destroyers of the original Carib or Indian of the country)
called together their chiefs, and giving them a treat in
the name of the King, explained to them the nature of
the oath of allegiance they had taken, and what was the
conduct expected from them, which they promised faithfully to pursue.

That it is apprehended from the very period of their promise, they considered merely how with safety to infringe it; their character of perfidy and deception on the late unhappy occasion, being masked by the most fair and delusive language and conduct to the British colonists in Saint Vincent, when they were on the very eve of setting forth to devastate all property, and declaredly to massacre and extirpate every English white inhabitant.

That this they unfortunately accomplished to a great degree, on the richest and most extensive part of the island, to the great grief of your Memorialists, from the murder of their friends and negroes, and to their utter ruin, if not assisted in the settlement of their estates, by benevolent measures adequate in their case, to be adopted in this country.

That above all, such re-settlement will not be practicable, or cannot be adopted, or pursued, with credit from the British merchants, or with general safety to your Memorialists, if the African negroes (usurping the Indian name of Caribs) are permitted to remain on the island; and they humbly call to the recollection of His Majesty's Ministers, the original plan of transporting them to a part of the world congenial to their origin, temper, and customs, has become indispensable to the safety of your Memorialists who have colonized and settled the most beautiful and fertile island of Saint Vincent by purchase from Government, and with much loyalty, industry, and exertion, a benefit, which as they humbly conceive, admits as little of comparison in point of justice, as of competition in point of national service, when contrasted with the conduct of those they plead the alternative of banishment against; for if these Africans remain your Memorialists must be driven from the island. The great losses your Memorialists have suffered in their fortunes, and the considerable loss of public revenue, they will presume humbly to state for consideration when more accurate details arrive; but they could not in justice to themselves, their friends, and their country, omit taking the very first and earliest occasion of soliciting the attention of His Majesty's Ministers to the conduct of the Black Caribs, and for such measures to be taken respecting those people as the wisdom of His Majesty's Councils shall deem right and proper.

WILLIAM YOUNG, Chairman.*

London, May 9, 1795.

* Sir William Young, Bart. proprietor of the Villa and Pembroke Estates in St. Vincent, afterwards Governor of Tobago, died there 1815.

No. XVI.

Apportionment of the Carib Lands, granted in Occupancies by Governor Henry William Bentinck.

No.	Original Occupants.	No. of Acres.	Present Estates.
1	William Gilchrist - -	174	⎫
2	W. Alexander and W. Coningham	276	⎪
3	Mount William - -	100	⎪
4	John Smith and Thomas Dakins	251	⎬ Grand Sable.
5	Samuel Reading - -	100	⎪
6	John Maxwell . -	100	⎪
7	James Gerald Morgan - -	300	⎭
8	Sebastian French - -	300	Mount Bentinck.
9	Thomas Dickson - -	101	Thomas Dickson.
10	Robert Brown - • -	350	Mount Bentinck.
11	John Cruikshank - -	600	Langley Park.
12	John Smith - -	310	Rabacca.
13	T. Patterson and W. M'Kenzie	300	Waterloo.
14	Alexander Cruikshank - -	300	Lot 14.
15	Robert Sutherland - -	300	Orange Hill.
16	John Kean - - -	300	Turama.
17	Akey Lawrence - - -	200	God Save the King.
18	Andrew Ross - - -	300	Turama.
19	Alexander Cumming - -	100	Lot 14.
20	John Brown - - -	100	Mount Bentinck.
21	John Prest - - -	100	Rabacca.
22	William Sterch - • -	100	Lot 14.
23	Thomas Hammond - -	200	Orange Hill and Waterloo.
		5,262	Acres.

No. XVII.

Appropriation of the Sum of £.25,000 granted to the Sufferers by the Volcanic Eruption by 53d Geo. III. Cap. 136.

		Estimated Loss.		Amount Sterling Paid.	
		£.	*s.*	*£,*	*s.*
Robert Sutherland for	Rabacca	19,378	0	5,300	0
John and Lewis Grant for	Wallibo	8,261	0	3,900	0
Charles Thesiger for	Duvallies	7,800	0	3,750	0
John Cruikshank for	Langley Park	8,064	0	2,400	0
Alex. Cruikshank and Alex. Cumming for	Lot 14	6,974	0	2,100	0
Thomas Browne for	Grand Sable	7,392	0	1,580	0
John Smith and Alex. Cumming for	Rabacca	4,780	0	1,200	0
William M'Kenzie for	Turama	4,006	0	1,140	0
Robert Brown for	Mount Bentinck	3,718	10	793	0
Thomas Fraser for	Frasers	1,262	0	700	0
James Cruikshank for	Richmond	3,528	0	654	0
John Low		378	10	200	0
Thomas Dickson		577	0	200	0
Jane Dermot		508	0	200	0
John W. Carmichael		820	0	180	0
Henry Haffey		1,100	5	166	0
Fanny Cruikshank		150	0	60	0
Thomas Riddock		75	0	57	7
Alexander Clunes		250	0	50	0
Henry Charles		103	0	50	0
				24,680	7
Treasury Charges and Commissions		-	-	319	13
		79,125	5	25,000	0

No. XVIII.

Abstract of the Slave Act, passed 16th December, 1825.
(See the Laws, Vol. II. page 249.)

I.
II.
III. } Slaves are declared real estate, and widows dowable, but they may be sold on deficiency of assets. Executors may advance money for payment of legacies to remain a charge on estates to prevent Slaves being sold.

IV. Free coloured persons not deemed Freeholders.

V. VI. } Slaves protected in the enjoyment of personal property.

VII. No shops to be kept open on Sundays.

VIII. } Slaves to be taught the principles of religion, and baptized gratis.

IX. Sunday Markets after ten o'clock abolished.

X. Marriages of Slaves encouraged.

XI.
XII.
XIII.
XIV. } No mills to be worked between seven o'clock on Saturday evening and four o'clock on Monday morning. Time for meals to be allowed, and sufficiency of land for provisions. Three holidays at Christmas, and Medical attendance.

XV. Diseased Slaves not to be suffered to wander.

XVI.
XVII. } Rewards paid for the rearing of children, and mothers having six children exempted from hard labour.

XVIII. } Manumissions to be recorded on payment of four pounds. Infirm slaves not to be manumitted.

XIX. } Detaining free persons in slavery provided against.

XX. Killing a Slave declared felony:

XXI.
XXII.
XXIII.
XXIV. } No Slave to receive more than ten stripes, and a book for the record of punishments to be kept on every estate; the use of the cart-whip abolished; and no chains to be used without a magistrate's license.

XXV.
XXVI. } Improper confinement or punishment of Slaves to be investigated by two justices, and redressed.

XXVII. } The detention of Slaves from their owners remedied; also the enticing and carrying away Slaves.

XXXI. XXXII.
XXXIII. XXXIV.
XXXV. XXXVI.
XXXVII. } Any Slave absent from the estate forty-eight hours, a runaway; the harbour-ing them punished; and the mode of proceeding against runaways.

XXXVIII.
XXXIX.
XL. XLI.
XLII. } Incorrigible runaways, or those going off the island, or stealing boats, deemed guilty of felony; also per-sons aiding, and accessories, may be proceeded against before the principals.

XLIII.
XLIV. } Freedom claimed by runaways to be investigated by three magistrates, and not to be sold without their certificate.

XLV.
XLVI. } No Slave to travel without a ticket, except to market; and the improper use of them prevented.

XLVII. } Slaves killed in the pursuit of runaways paid for.

XLVIII.
XLIX. } Nightly meetings of Slaves after ten o'clock restrained, and free persons attending or permitting them fined.

L. LI. } Slaves forming camps, administering unlawful oaths, or learning the use of arms, guilty of felony.

LII. ⎫⎬⎭ Having arms in their possession, with evil intent, punishable by transportation or imprisonment.

LIII. ⎫
LIV. ⎬ Obeah practices declared felony.
LV. ⎭

LVI. ⎱ Slaves preaching subjected to corporal punish-ment.

LVII. ⎫⎬⎭ Taking twenty shillings by force, or break-ing open a building, or stealing six pounds, declared felony.

LVIII. Striking white or free persons also a felony.

LIX. ⎱ Using defamatory language punished by whipping.

LX. ⎱ Slaves maiming Slaves so as to endanger life, a felony.

LXI. Slaves fighting punished by whipping.

LXII. ⎫
LXIII. ⎬ Stealing cattle a felony; having meat in their possession, and using cruelty towards cattle
LXIV. ⎭ punishable by whipping or imprisonment.

LXV. Clearing ground by fire, restrained.

LXVI. ⎫⎬⎭ Evidence of Slaves in criminal cases (except against their owners) admitted under re-strictions, and subpœnas to be directed to
LXVII. their owners.

LXVIII. ⎫
LXIX. ⎬ Slaves to be punished for all crimes the same as white persons; when tried, to be defended by counsel, and if executed, or condemned for transportation, to be paid for by the
LXX. ⎭ public; the fees to be the same as free persons.

LXXI. ⎱ All other misdemeanours and false evidence
LXXII. ⎰ to be tried by two justices.

LXXIII. ⎫
LXXIV. ⎪
LXXV. ⎪ Slaves to be sold for transportation by the Marshal, a purchaser to give bond for their removal, and make oath to transport them;
LXXVI. ⎬ if found at large to be resold, and return from transportation deemed a felony, and
LXXVII. ⎪ the bringing them back punishable by fine
LXXVIII. ⎪ and imprisonment.
LXXIX. ⎭

LXXX.   The only mode of execution to be by hanging.

LXXXI.
LXXXII. } Buying sugar or other prohibited articles or stolen goods from Slaves, punishable by fine or imprisonment.

LXXXIII. } Conviction of a misdemeanour a bar to prosecution for being accessary to a felony.

LXXXIV. } Selling strong liquors to Slaves, or permitting gambling, punished by fine, and whipping of the Slave.

LXXXV.
LXXXVI.
LXXXVII. } Warrants for Slaves to be served on their owners, and to be executed by constables, and not to be refused by magistrates.

LXXXVIII.
LXXXIX.
XC.   } The fees to be the same as in other cases, and in cases of poverty to be paid by the public. The fines to be recovered by warrant, and paid to the treasury for the public use.

XCI.   } This Act to be in force for seven years, from 16th December, 1825.

No. XIX.

Militia Commissions, as renewed every seven years under the Acts.

1787.

SOUTHERN REGIMENT.

George Lowman, Colonel.
John Greatheed, Lieut. Colonel.
James Hartley, Major.

CAPTAINS.

Jonas Akers.
Richard J. Whyttel.
David Miller.

William Greig.
Gilbert Douglas.

LIEUTENANTS.

Gilbert Gollan.
*Jonathan Morgan.
Robert E. Henville.

Farquhar Campbell.
Edward French.

ENSIGNS.

William Hepburn.
Thomas Morgan.
Charles M. Henville.

John Glover.
Daniel Macdowall.
Herbert P. Cox, Adjutant.

TROOP OF LIGHT CAVALRY.

Andrew Ross, Captain and Lieut. Colonel.
Luke R. Phipps, } Lieutenants.
John Brown, }
John Cruikshank, Cornet.

NORTHERN REGIMENT.

Robert Wynne, Colonel.
Peter Haffey, Lieut. Colonel.
Robert Gordon, Major.

CAPTAINS.

John Kearton.
James G. Morgan.
Thomas Bruce.

William Doyle.
Andrew Ross.

* Officer living.

g

APPENDIX.

No. XIX. *continued.*

LIEUTENANTS.

James Buchan.   Charles Grant.
Alexander Leith.   James Campbell.
Josias Jackson.

ENSIGNS.

John White.   Michael Keane.
George Hepburn.   William Taylor, Adjutant.
Robert Robinson.

QUEEN'S COMPANIES.

CAPTAIN.

Alexander B. Irwin.

LIEUTENANTS.

Samuel B. Windsor.   John Macdowall.

ENSIGN.

James D. Questell.

Judge Advocate. * John Wilson.

1799.

SOUTHERN REGIMENT.

* Henry Haffey, Colonel.
Andrew Ross, Lieut. Colonel.
Sebastian French, Major.

CAPTAINS.

William Hepburn.   * Warner Ottley.
Daniel Macdowall.   * Alexander Cruikshank.
Thomas Patterson.   William M'Kenzie.
Robert Lauder.   Thomas Slater.
Edward Jackson.   Herbert P. Cox, Adjutant.

LIEUTENANTS

Robert Gibson.   Charles Lacroix.
James Ruddoch.   A. Dubois.
* George Hartley.   * John Cropper.
* Gilbert Munro.   Thomas Hatton.

• Officers living.

No. XIX. *continued.*

ENSIGNS.

Robert Sutherland.
* Alexander Cumming.
W. H. Durham.
* David Boyd.
George Burgess.
* John Roche Dasent.

George Sutton.
R. Watkinson.
John Lowe.
* William Durham.
* John Herbert, Surgeon.
Colin Dallas, Assistant Surgeon.

William Hodge, Quarter Master.

NORTHERN REGIMENT.

Robert Gordon, Colonel.
Peter Gurley, Lieut. Colonel.
John Cruikshank, Major.

CAPTAINS.

George Hepburn.
Walter Morrison.
Robert Douglas.

John Coupland.
Thomas Fraser.

LIEUTENANTS.

* Macduff Fyfe.
John Murray.

Andrew M'Craken.
James Rickard.

ENSIGNS.

* Richard Nichol.
John Lowry.

Leonard H. Dunlop.
* Patrick Rickard.

* Joseph Billinghurst, Adjutant.
* Thomas Smith, Surgeon.
H. Gardiner, Assistant Surgeon.
William Llewellyn, Quarter Master.

1806.

TROOP OF LIGHT CAVALRY.

James M'Caul, Major.
————————, Captain.
George Maitland, Lieutenant.
*P. M. Lucas, Cornet.

SOUTHERN REGIMENT.

* Henry Haffey, Colonel.
Daniel Macdowall, Lieut. Colonel.
Edward Jackson, Major.

* Officers living.

No. XIX. *continued.*

CAPTAINS.

* Warner Ottley.
William M'Kenzie.
Thomas Slater.
H. P. Cox, Adjutant.
* William John Struth.

* George Hartley.
James Lacroix.
* John Cropper.
William H. Durham.
* David Boyd.

LIEUTENANTS.

* John R. Dasent.
* William Durham.
Thomas Hammond.
* N. B. Cropper.
* James Grant,
* Joseph Billinghurst.

John Grant.
Nathaniel Taynton.
Charles Grant, junior.
* William Taylor, junior.
George Aberdeen.
* Ashton Warner.

ENSIGNS.

Joseph Stowe.
* James Douglas.
James Steele.
James Mahon.
Colin Dallas, Assist. Surgeon.

James Coram.
* J. F. Trimingham.
John Clarke, Quarter Master.
* John Herbert, Surgeon.
Alex. Rimia, Paymaster.

NORTHERN REGIMENT.

Robert Gordon, Colonel.
Walter Morrison, Lieut. Colonel.
John Coupland, Major.

CAPTAINS.

Thomas Fraser.
* M'Duff Fyfe.

Andrew M'Crachan.
Leo. H. Dunlop.

LIEUTENANTS,

* Patrick Rickard.
John Smith, Adjutant.
James Buchan.

* Robert Hares.
Patrick Murray.

ENSIGNS.

William Patterson.
Francis W. Ward.

Patrick Cruikshank.

* Thomas Smith, Surgeon.
Simon Armstrong, Assistant Surgeon.
James M. Grant, Paymaster.

* Officers living.

No. XIX. *continued.*

QUEEN'S COMPANIES.

CAPTAINS.

* James Huggins.   James D. Questel.

LIEUTENANTS.

* William M'Gowne.   * Harry Hackshaw.

ENSIGNS.

Charles Macdowall.   John Smyth.
* Allan Macdowall, Surgeon.
S. B. Windsor, Judge Advocate.

1814.

TROOP OF LIGHT CAVALRY.

Richard Rees, Major Commanding.
John P. Ross, Captain.
† James Adams, Lieutenant.
Daniel Wall, Surgeon.

SOUTHERN REGIMENT.

† Daniel Macdowall, Colonel.
† Edward Jackson, Lieut. Colonel.
George Hartley, Major.

CAPTAINS.

† Herbert P. Cox, Adjutant.   † James Steele.
James Grant.   John F. Trimingham.
Joseph Billinghurst.   John Prest.
† John Grant.   † John Johnson.
† William Taylor.   † John Luke.

LIEUTENANTS.

Horatio N. Huggins.   † John Dalzell.
† James Cruikshank.   William H. Prescod.
William Laborde.   Charles Conyers.
† James Punnett.   † Daniel Brown.
John George Nanton.   John M'Lean.
Duncan Brown.

* Officers living.   † Officers deceased.

No. XIX. *continued.*

ENSIGNS.

* John Waterston.   Joseph Lewis.
P. S. Moore.   James Hutcheon.
* James M'Leod.   John Small.
Richard Arundell, Surgeon.
John Carsley, Assistant Surgeon.
William Game, Quarter Master.

NORTHERN REGIMENT.

* Robert Gordon, Colonel.
M'Duff Fyfe, Lieut. Colonel.
* John Smith, Major.

CAPTAINS.

Robert Hares.   * Hugh Lennox.
* F. William Waid.   Thomas Wilkinson.

LIEUTENANTS.

John Rickard.   * Charles Slater.
* John Dallaway.   William Hepburn.
* William Malcolm, Adjutant.

ENSIGNS.

James Wilson.   * Robert Dalzell.
* Charles M. Spence.   Edward Rees.
Thomas Smith, Surgeon.
* Simon Armstrong, Assist. Surgeon.
* John Gaskill, Quarter Master.

QUEEN'S COMPANIES.

* James D. Questel, Lieut. Colonel Commanding.

CAPTAINS.

Harry Hackshaw.   William M'Gowne.
* Charles Macdowall.

LIEUTENANTS.

* John Smyth.   Kenneth Ross.
Patrick Crichton.

* Officers deceased.

No. XIX. *continued.*

ENSIGNS.

Thomas Dickson.   James Sutherland.
Allan Macdowall, Surgeon.
Daniel Huggins, Assistant Surgeon.
* William Cotton, ⎫
* Francis Brown, ⎬ Quarter Masters.

1821.

TROOP OF LIGHT CAVALRY.

James W. Brown, Major Commanding.
John Ponsonby, Captain.
John D. Beresford, Lieutenant.
Thomas Le Gall, Cornet.
Solomon G. Warner, Surgeon.

SOUTHERN REGIMENT.

* Edward Jackson, Colonel.
* Joseph Billinghurst, Lieut. Colonel.
J. F. Trimingham, Major.

CAPTAINS.

* H. P. Cox, Adjutant.   William H. Prescod.
John Prest.   John M'Lean.
* James Punnett.   P. S. Moore.
Duncan Brown.   * James M'Leod.
* John Dalzell.   Joseph Lewis.

LIEUTENANTS.

John Small.   John Denton.
* William Thomson.   Roger Woodburne.
William Rose Scott.   Adam Boyd.
Alexander Small.   Isaac Arrindell.
* James Wyllie.   John D. Crawford.
Robert Gaskill.   Josias Huson.

ENSIGNS.

John M'Arthur.   Joseph Huggins.
Barnewall Jackson.   Daniel V. Seymour.
George R. Darrell.   Duncan F. Sutherland.
* Thomas James Smith, Surgeon.
* Alexander Mackie, Quarter Master.

* Officers deceased.

No. XIX. *continued.*

NORTHERN REGIMENT.

John Smith, Colonel.
Robert Hares, Lieut. Colonel.
Thomas Wilkinson, Major.

CAPTAINS.

* William Malcolm, Adjutant. Edward Rees
* Charles Spence.   Evan Stephei
* Robert Dalzell.

LIEUTENANTS.

Thomas Jeffers.   John Wiseman.
Robert Russell.   John Clarke.

ENSIGNS.

* John S. Spence.   Alexander Smart.
Bentinck Gurley.   Francis John Eve.
* James Mitchell, Quarter Master.
* Patrick Murray, Surgeon.

QUEEN'S COMPANIES.

Harry Hackshaw, Major Commanding.

CAPTAINS.

Patrick Crichton, Adjutant. James Sutherland.
Thomas Dickson.

LIEUTENANTS.

Roger Swire.   William Sprott.

ENSIGNS.

Alexander M'Leod.   * John Dickie.
John George Cox, Quarter Master.
Daniel Huggins, Surgeon.
John Melville, Surgeon.
Pemberton Hobson, Judge Advocate.

* Officers deceased.

No. XIX. *continued.*

1828.

Troop of Light Cavalry.

* Sir Charles Brisbane, Colonel.
James William Brown, Major Commanding.
* Robert Dalzell, Captain.
George Power, Cornet.
Thomas H. Dakins, Surgeon.

SOUTHERN REGIMENT.

* John Dalzell, Colonel.
William T. Dickinson, Lieut. Colonel.
William Rose Scott, Major.

Captains.

John P. Ross.	Robert Gaskill.
John Prest, Adjutant.	Alexander Small.
John M'Lean.	Nathan Newbold.
William Boyd.	Adam Boyd.
William Laborde.	

Lieutenants.

* Daniel Brown.	John Primrose.
John M'Arthur.	Adam Skelly.
Josias Huson.	William Edgar.
Barnwell Jackson.	Henry Trimingham.
George R. Darrell.	William Hopley.
Francis John Eve.	Nathaniel Trimingham.
Benj. F. Hutchins.	

Arthur Wall, Surgeon.
Robert C. West, Quarter Master.

KING'S COMPANIES.

Robert Hares, Colonel Commanding.
Alexander M'Barnet, Major.

Captains.

Evan Stephens.	Robert Russell.

* Officers deceased.

No. XIX. *continued.*

LIEUTENANTS.

Charles D. Horne.   John Gordon.

ENSIGNS.

Christopher Punnett, jun^r.   William Hunt.
Bentinck Gurley, Adjutant.
John Horne, Quarter Master.

QUEEN'S COMPANIES.

Patrick Crichton, Major Commanding.

CAPTAINS.

James Sutherland.   William Sprott.
Alexander M'Leod, Adjutant.

LIEUTENANTS.

John George Cox.   James Donelan.

ENSIGNS.

John Carmichael.   John Jennings.
* Alexander Patterson, Quarter Master.
Pemberton Hobson, Judge Advocate.

* Officers deceased.

No. XX.

References to the Plan of the Island, as published by John Byres, in 1776.

Lot.	Original Purchasers.	Acres.	Present Estates.
1	Fitzhugh	223	Richmond Vale.
2	Fenner	24	Unoccupied.
3	} Millingtons - -{	51	} Bostock Park.
4		91	
5	Hunt	59	
6	Kladen	137	} Petit Bordell.
7	Poor Settlers	65	
8	Barrack Ground	13	Golden Grove.
9	Poor Settlers	40	Fraser's.
10	} Connor -{	44	} Unoccupied.
11		73	
12	Hamilton	22	Bostock Park.
13	Laudaux	20	Bostock Park.
14	Galle	14	} Golden Grove.
15	Gressier	17	
16	Mocquet	50	} Mount Alexander.
17	Twerts	62	
18	Sharpe	42	Sharpe's.
19	Akers	31	Mount Alexander.
20	} Ottley and Abel -{	57	} Bostock Park.
21		64	
22		63	
23	Doile	44	Golden Grove.
24	Dominique Valideris	50	Richmond.
25	Audibert	43	Mount Alexander.
26	Howard	68	} Rose Bank.
27	Bell	60	
28	St. Lawrence	95	Belmont.
29	Porter	42	} Bostock Park.
30	Jameson	62	
31	Sharpe	49	
32	Ingram	57	Unoccupied.
33	Kegan	40	Convent.
34	Hyndeman and Boyle	400	Unoccupied.

No. XX. *continued.*

Lot.	Original Purchasers.	Acres.	Present Estates.
35 36	} Gordon {	49 98	} Spring Estate.
37	Patullo	95	Spring Estate.
38	White	204	Belle-isle.
39	Patullo	124	Mount Hope.
40	Sharpe	74	Bostock Park.
41	Coram	39	Belmont.
42 43	} Millington {	60 112	} Millington's.
44	Hawkes	38	Westwood.
45	Coram	42	Cumberland & Westwood.
46	Armstrong & Taylor	58	L'Ance Mahaut.
47	Nichols	48	Wallilabo.
48	White	67	Belle-isle.
49	Gumbs and Milliard	314	Wallilabo.
50	Morgan and Lawley	84	} Kearton's.
51	Lindow	123	
52	Russell	193	Reversion.
53	Gurley	83	} Peter's Hope.
54	Ashe	54	
55	Fletcher and Glover	72	Reversion.
56	{ Fletcher, Nugent, and Gurley }	198	} Peter's Hope.
57	Wynne	181	Mount Wynne.
58	De la Caze	43	Rutland Vale.
59	Clapham	5	Rutland Vale.
60	Coram	110	Bell Wood.
61	Clapham	56	} Palmiste.
62	Bonnet	18	
63	Haffey	55	
64	Jackson	110	} Rutland Vale.
65	Clapham	38	
66	Jackson	46	
67	Akers	19	Akers' Layou.
68 69	} Jackson {	34 53	Bonaventure. Rutland Vale.
70	Armstrong & Taylor	9	Cumberland.
71	White	27	Belle-isle.

No. XX. *continued.*

Lot.	Original Purchasers.	Acres.	Present Estates.
72	} Jackson	15	Rutland Vale.
73		37	Belle-isle.
74		57	Mount Wynne.
75		68	Peter's Hope.
76	Poor Settlers.	125	Wallilabo.
77		60	Belle-isle.
78		141	Several Estates.
79		107	Cumberland & Westwood.
80	Wynne	19	Mount Wynne.
81	Wilmot	80	Belmont
82	Reed	123	L'Ance Mahaut.
83	Hawkes	7	Westwood.
84	White	70	} Belle-isle.
85	Jackson	30	
86	M'Dowal, Thompson, and Bruce	12	Convent.
87	Bruce and Gordon	52	Grove.
88	Braham	7	Reversion.
89	Campbell	167	} Unoccupied.
90	Poor Settlers	630	
91	Antoine Marchais	12	Cumberland.
92	George Kearton	23	Kearton's.
93	Yeamans	382	} Queensbury.
94	Stephens	74	
95	Gumbes	338	Retreat.
96	Pennistons	208	Pennistons.
97	Hackshaw	212	Hope.
98	North of Queen's River, Sir William Young	296	N. Queensbury.
98	South of Queen's River, ditto.	183	Pembroke.
99	St. Lawrence	207	
100	Ottley	248	} Cane Grove.
101	Passey	103	
102	Mallony	19	Queensbury.
103	Hendy	198	} Clare Valley.
104	Gilbert	52	

No. XX. *continued.*

Lot.	Original Purchasers.	Acres.	Present Estates.
105	Hunt - -	203	Cane Wood.
106	Kennedy - -	122	
107	Burton and Payne -	70	
108	Sharpe - -	276	Camden Park.
109	Ingram - -	126	Ottley Hall.
110	Alexander - -	382	Redemption and Liberty Lodge.
111		83	Montrose.
112	Smith - -	59	Redemption.
113	Sharpe - -	50	
114	Becket - -	85	
115	Blair and Co. -	138	Richmond Hill.
116	Keane - -	45	M. Gumbs'.
117	Lowman - -	8	Camden Park.
118	Alexander - -	42	Montrose.
119	French - -	4	Richmond Hill.
120	Sommersall -	121	
121	French - -	3	
122	Lee - - -	50	Cane Garden.
123	Davies - -	74	Sion Hill.
124	Jackson - -	62	Cane Hall and Sion Hill.
125	Crooke and Greatheed	350	Arno's Vale.
126	Jackson - -	111	Cane Hall.
127	Fenner - -	20	
128	Bowles - -	134	Strowan Cottage.
129	Mackie - -	126	Fountain and Bellair.
130	Jackson - -	42	Cane Hall.
131	Nanton - -	274	Villa Estate.
132	Brebner - -	177	Fairhall.
133	Yeamans - -	26	Harmony Hall.
134	Crooke - -	83	
135		22	Golden Vale.
136	Wilkie - -	121	Ratho Mill.
137	Yeamans - -	147	Prospect.
138	Geffrier - -	2	Belvidere.
139	Lawley - -	39	Lower Diamond.
140	Lawley and Morgan	292	Upper & Lower Diamond.
141	Hyndman and Boyle	221	Brighton.

No. XX. *continued.*

Lot.	Original Purchasers.	Acres.	Present Estates.
142	Brebner - -	98	Revolution Hall.
143	Nanton - -	7	Villa.
144	Byres - -	471	Belmont and Golden Vale.
145	Baker and Collins -		Cane Hall.
146	Sir William Young	16	Villa.
147	Alexander - ..	25	Montrose.
148	Cooke and Greatheed	31	Arno's Vale.
149	Kair - - -	104	Cubaimaróu.
150	Gilbert - -	2	Taylor's Lot.
151	Walker and Atkinson	17	Kingstown Park.
152	} Poor Settlers. - {	64	{ Anderson's Lot.
153		240	Cane Garden, part of Orange Grove, &c.
154	Church & Churchyard	5	Golden Vale.
155	{ Reserved for Military purposes -		} Golden Grove.
156	Poor Settlers - }	53	
157	Ditto - - -		Unoccupied.
158	Churchyard -		Churchyard.
159	Barrack Ground -	50	Reversion.
160	Parsonage - -		Parsonage.
161			} Queensbury.
162		95	
163	} Poor Settlers {	109	Unoccupied.
164		32	Akers' Layou.
165		124	Clare Valley.
166	Garden Lots -		Montrose.
167	{ Lieut. Governor's House & Ground }	40	} Kingstown Park.
168	Garden Lots -		Sion Hill.
169	} Poor Settlers - - {	50	Montrose, and Botanical Garden.
170		10	Botanical Garden.
171	Young's Island -		Villa.

No. XX. *continued.*

Lands leased to the French Inhabitants, distinguished by an Asterisk annexed to the figure.

Lot.	Original Lessees.	Acres.	Present Estates.
1	Heude -	51	Richmond and Fitzhughs.
2	Arsoneau - -	112	Fraser's and Fitzhughs.
3	} Galle - - - {	15	} Golden Grove.
4		6	
5	Bruard - -	8	Riddocks.
6	Galle - - -	10	Golden Grove.
7	Pereau - -	10	Fitzhughs.
8	Gressier - -	17	Golden Grove.
9	Heude - -	15	Richmond.
10	Breun - -	39	Golden Grove.
11	Heirs of Mocquet -	31	} Mount Alexander.
12	Audibert - -	42	
13	Twerts - -	36	
14	} Mocquet - - {	31	} Sharpes and Mount Alexander.
15			
16	Disord - -	49	Golden Grove.
17	Godin - -	15	Sharpes.
18	Divizien - -	16	Bostock Park.
19	La Croix - -	8	Rose Bank.
20	Mocquet - -	38	Sharpes.
21	Gayrin - -	41	Troumaca.
22	} Marchais - - {	76	} Bostock, Spring, and Westwood.
23	Tetron - -	64	Spring.
24	De Colval - -	42	Grove.
25	Michelle - -	135	Belmont.
26	Marquiees - -	62	Westwood.
27	Gayrin - -	21	} Troumaca.
28	Gaye -	18	
29	Greaux - -	20	Westwood.
30	Valle - -	50	Cumberland.
31	Temple - -	10	Unoccupied.
32	Valle - -	21	L'Ance Mahaut.
33	Marchais - -	17	Cumberland.

No. XX. *continued.*

Lot.	Original Lessees.	Acres.	Present Estates.
34	Blee - - -	14	Spring.
35	Dumay - -	11	Grove.
36	} La Roche. - -{	29	} Belleisle.
37		17	
38		37	
39	Dumay - -	49	
40	Castillon - -	19	
41	} Burgros - -{	37	
42		22	Keartons.
43	} Heude - -{	50	Keartons.
44		18	Robert Hares.
45		19	
46	Desbat - -	38	} Peter's Hope.
47	De la Tour - -	28	
48	Rhoderiques -	31	} Mount Wynne.
49	Saidre - -	10	
50	Greaux - -	10	
51	} La Roche - -}	9	
52		10	
53	La Caze and Cherpy	110	
54	Papin - -	85	Bellwood.
55	Bonnet - -	10	Palmiste.
56	Riviere - -	55	} Rutland Vale.
57	Goodraw - -	84	
58	} Papin - -{	36	} Rutland Vale and the Heirs of H. P. Cox.
59	La Roche - -	33	} Rutland Vale.
60	Tetron - -	10	
61	Greaux - -	29	
62	Prevot - -	37	
63	Ville - -	10	
64	Guilleau - -	10	
65	D'Huet - -	10	
66	La Caze and Cherpy	16	
67	Saidre - -	10	
68	Prevot - -	50	Akers' Layou.
69	La Caze and Cherpy	22	} Rutland Vale.
70	Anoine - -	10	

No. XX. *continued.*

Lot.	Original Lessees.	Acres.	Present Estates.
71	Imbert - -	5	} Rutland Vale.
72	Porierer - -	10	
73	Texier - -	43	
74	La Croix - -	14	Bostock Park.
75	Bonamy and Mondesir	222	Pembroke.
76	Mullony - -	47	} Queensbury.
77	Dubois - -	69	
78	Questell - -	177	Lance Joyeuse.
79	Aulemon - -	52	Camden Park.
80	Le Fort - -	19	{ New Edinburgh, and Ottley Hall.
81	Marin - -	28	Kingstown Park.
82	La Cavalrie -	38	Sundry Occupants.
83	} Delzien - - {	64	Kingstown Park.
84		53	Montrose.
85	Constantine -	13	} Sion Hill.
86	Laborde - -	38	
87	Flanarins - -	22	Cane Garden.
88	La Ford - -	29	Sion Hill.
89	Rigaud - -	32	Cane Hall.
90	La Croix - -	21	Retreat.
91	Dubois - -	18	} Cane Hall.
92	La Taste - -	66	
93	Pradie, Senior -	49	Revolution Hall.
94	Lewis Pradie -	72	{ Arrendell, Brown and Nanton.
95	Le Metre - -	6	
96	Riviere - -	16	Fountain.
97	Marginiere and Co.	42	Revolution Hall.
98	Dariex - -	44	Belmont.
99	Marginiere - -	38	Carapan.
100	Levat - -	28	} Fairhall.
101	Duplessis - -	81	
102	Campouse - -	35	Belvidere.
103	Riviere - -	19	} Revolution Hall.
104	Bertage - -	22	
105	Raquet - -	41	
106	Constant - -	45	

No. XX. *continued.*

Lot.	Original Lessees.	Acres.	Present Estates.
107	Marginiere - -	9	Revolution Hall.
108	Pradie, Senior -	115	} Golden Vale.
109	Lefort - -	9	
110	Tonnant and Honzale	37	Belvidere.
111	Imbert - -	74	Ratho Mill, and Prospect.
112	Geffrier - -	100	Belvidere.
113	Clouet - -	35	} Ratho Mill.
114	Arnaud - -	15	

No. XXI.

A Chronology of the most remarkable Events relative to the West Indies.

	A. D.
Columbus discovered the first land, Guanahane, now St. Salvador, October 10th, - - -	1492
——————— Cuba, October 27th, Hispaniola, November 22nd, - - - -	..
——————— Dominica, Guadaloupe, & Porto Rico - - - - -	1493
——————— Jamaica, May 3rd, - -	1494
——————— Saint Vincent, Grenada, and Trinidad - - - - -	1498
——————— Porto Bello and Veragua -	1503
Columbus died May 20th, - - - -	1506
Saint Eustatia occupied by the Dutch - -	1600
Barbados discovered - - - -	1608
Saint Christopher settled by Thomas Warner -	1623
Barbados settled by Sir William Courteen - -	1624
Santa Crux settled by the English and Dutch -	1625
Berbice colonised by the Dutch - - -	1626
Providence, in the Bahamas, settled - -	1629
Antigua and Montserratt settled by Sir Thomas Warner - - - - -	1632
Curaçoa taken possession of by the Dutch -	1634
Guadaloupe and Martinique colonised by the French	1635

No. XXI. *continued.*

	A. D.
Saint Lucia surrendered to Lord Willoughby -	1639
Sugar first made in Barbados - - -	1640
Quinquina (Jesuit's Bark) first carried to Europe -	..
Surinam abandoned by the French and occupied by the English - - - - -	1641
A hurricane - - - - -	1642
The Dutch expelled the French from Cayenne -	1646
Grenada taken possession of by M. Du Parquet	1650
Saint Lucia occupied by the French - - -	..
Anguilla colonised by the English - - -	..
Wars between the Caribs and the French settlers -	1655
The Cocoa-tree first discovered in Martinico -	..
Jamaica conquered by the British under Venables and Penn - - - - - -	..
Hurricane at Guadaloupe - - - -	1656
Earthquake at Martinico - - -	1657
The Caribs driven out of Martinico - -	1658
A Treaty between the English, French, and Caribs, leaving the latter undisturbed possession of Dominica and Saint Vincent, March 31st, - -	1660
The first settlement of Campeachy - -	1662
The 4½ per Cent. Act passed in Barbados, September 12th, - - - -	1663
Lord Willoughby obtained a Grant of Antigua	..
French West India Company formed - -	1664
The first General Assembly at Jamaica ,	..
Lord Willoughby, and 15 sail, lost in a hurricane off Guadaloupe, August 4th, - - -	1666
Montserratt taken by the French - - -	1667
Treaty of Buda signed, the English half of Saint Christophers, Antigua, and Montserrat restored to the English, July 21st, - - -	..
New Providence in the Bahamas settled - -	..
Bridge Town, Barbados, destroyed by fire -	1668
The cultivation of Sugar commenced in Antigua by Colonel Codrington - - -	1674
The French West India Company dissolved, and the Islands annexed to the Crown - -	..
Hurricane at Barbados, August 10th, - -	1675
A Slave-ship wrecked on Bequia; the crew got to Saint Vincent, and were there joined by runaways from other Islands - - -	..
Coffee first cultivated in Jamaica, - -	1676

No. XXI. *continued.*

No. XXI. *continued.*

	A. D.
Captain Woods Rogers subdues the Pirates at the Bahamas - - - -	1718
All the Cocoa-trees in Martinico destroyed by the wind - - - -	..
Major Paulian, with a French force from Martinico, landed in Saint Vincent to assist the Red Caribs against the Blacks, but was obliged to retreat -	1719
The Coffee-tree introduced at Cayenne from Surinam	1721
Port Royal, Jamaica, destroyed by a hurricane, Aug. 28th, - - - - -	1722
Saint Vincent and Saint Lucia granted to the Duke of Montague, by Letters Patent, June 22nd, -	..
Captain Brathwaite endeavoured to take possession of St. Vincent - - - -	1723
A hurricane at Jamaica, Oct. 22nd, - -	1726
Dr. Berkeley attempted to establish a College in Bermuda - - - -	1729
Saint Vincent, Saint Lucia, and Dominica declared neutral by the English and French - -	1730
The Moravians sent Missionaries to the West Indies	1732
Santa Crux sold by the French to the Danes for £75,000. - - - -	1733
A hurricane at Jamaica - - -	1734
A conspiracy to murder the Whites discovered at Antigua, and the ringleaders executed - -	1736
Hurricane at Saint Domingo, Saint Kitts and Montserratt - - - -	1737
Great losses sustained from the depredations committed by the Spanish Guard Costas - -	..
Pacification between the inhabitants of Jamaica and the Maroons - - - -	1738
War with Spain - - - -	1739
Porto Bello taken by Admiral Vernon - -	..
Spanish fleet destroyed off Boca Chica - -	1741
British settlement at Rattan established - -	1742
Guinea grass introduced in Jamaica from Africa	1744
Hurricane at Jamaica, October 20th, - -	..
Capture of French vessels by Admiral Townsend off Martinico - - - - -	1745
Admiral Hawke's Victory over the French fleet, October 14th, - - - -	1747
Two hurricanes among the Leeward Islands, September 21st and October 24th, - -	..

No. XXI. *continued.*

	A. D.
Treaty of Aix-la-Chapelle signed October 7th; Saint Vincent, Dominica, Tobago and Saint Lucia declared neutral, and to belong to the Caribs	1748
Admiral Knowles destroyed the Fort of Port Louis in St. Domingo - - - -	..
Peace between England and Spain -	1750
War between England and France -	1756
Fire at Bridgetown, Barbados, February 8th, -	..
British attack on Martinico, and Capture of Gaudaloupe - - - - -	1759
George III. acceded to the Throne -	1760
Insurrection in Jamaica - -	1760
First Methodist Meeting in the West Indies held at Antigua - - - -	..
Terms agreed to between the inhabitants of Surinam and the revolted Negroes - -	1761
Dominica taken by the English -	..
Martinico taken by Admiral Rodney and General Monckton, February 4th; also Grenada, Tobago, and Saint Vincent surrendered, -	1762
Saint Lucia taken, February 26th, -	
Capture of the Havanna, August 13th, -	..
Insurrection of the Negroes in Berbice -	1763
The Ants first appeared in Martinico; they had prevailed at Barbados some time before -	..
Peace of Paris, February 10th, - -	..
Gaudaloupe, Martinico, Saint Lucia surrendered to France; Saint Vincent, Grenada, Dominica, and Tobago to England, and the Havanna to Spain,	..
General Melville appointed to the Government of Saint Vincent, Grenada, Dominica and Tobago,	..
Saint Vincent Botanic Garden established -	..
The Duke of Montague's claim to Saint Vincent disallowed by the Privy Council - -	1764
Hurricane at Martinico and Gaudaloupe -	1765
Moravian Missionaries arrived at Barbados -	..
The First General Assembly called in Grenada; the payment of the 4½ per cent. duties resisted	..
Great fire at Bridgetown, Barbados, May 13, and again December 22d, - -	1766
Hurricane at Dominica, Martinico, Montserratt and St. Kitts, August and September, -	..
Earthquake in Jamaica - - -	..

No. XXI. *continued.*

	A. D.
The troops sent against runaway Slaves in Grenada	1767
Earthquake at Martinico - • -	..
Conspiracy at Montserratt discovered - -	1768
The Carib lands in Saint Vincent ordered to be surveyed and sold - - - -	..
Several estates burnt at Santa Crux, July 15th	..
Saint John's, Antigua, nearly destroyed by fire, August 17th, - - - -	1769
Dominica made a separate government - -	1770
Great earthquake at Saint Domingo, June 3d,	..
William Leyborne Leyborne, Governor of the Southern Caribbee Islands, May 2d, - - -	..
Saint George's, Grenada, destroyed by fire, December 27th, - - -	1771
Disputes in Saint Vincent between the Commissioners and the Caribs - - - -	..
Hurricane in the Leeward Islands - -	1772
Treaty of Peace between the English and the Caribs	1773
Judgment pronounced against the Claim of the Crown to the 4¼ per cent. duties in the ceded Islands	1774
Commencement of the American War - -	1775
Saint George's, Grenada, nearly destroyed by fire, November 1st, - - -	1776
Valentine Morris, Governor of Saint Vincent -	..
Dominica taken by the French, September 7th, -	1778
Saint Lucia taken by the English; Count Destaing repulsed, December 30th, - • -	..
Saint Vincent taken by the French, June 18th, -	1779
Grenada taken by the French, July 3d, - -	..
Great drought in Antigua - - -	..
Admiral Rodney's indecisive engagement with the French fleet, April 17th, - - -	1780
Great hurricane throughout the Islands, October	..
American Independency declared - -	..
Admiral Rodney and General Vaughan attempted to retake Saint Vincent - - -	..
Saint Eustatia taken by the English, February 3d,	1781
500 houses burnt in Rosseau, Dominica, Easter Sunday - - - -	..
Saint Eustatia and Saint Martin's retaken, Dec. 15th,	..
A hurricane at Jamaica, August 1st, - -	..
Tobago taken by the French, June 2d, - -	..

No. XXI. *continued.*

	A. D.
Saint Christophers taken by the French, February 13th ; Nevis and Montserratt also surrendered	1782
Admiral Rodney's Victory over the French Fleet, April 12th, - - - -	..
The Ramillies and several other Ships lost, July	..
The Mango, Cinnamon, and Mangosteen introduced at Jamaica by Lord Rodney - -	..
Peace between Great Britain and France, Jan. 28th,	1783
Saint Vincent, Grenada, Dominica and Saint Christopher, Nevis, and Montserratt ceded to Great Britain, Saint Lucia and Tobago to France -	..
Edmund Lincoln, Esq. appointed Governor of Saint Vincent, March 3d, - - -	..
Port au Prince, Saint Domingo, destroyed by Fire, June 29th, - . -	1784
Hurricane at Jamaica, July 30, - -	..
The Runaway Slaves in Dominica suppressed -	1785
Hurricane at Jamaica, Guadaloupe and Barbados, September and October, - - -	1786
First Wesleyan Missionaries in St. Vincent, Jan. 9th,	1787
James Seton, Esq. Governor of St. Vincent, April 2d,	..
Intended Insurrection in Demerary discovered,	1789
Great Losses in Antigua from want of Rain -	..
Commencement of the Troubles in Saint Domingo,	..
Ogè and Chavanne executed at St. Domingo, March,	1790
Great Flood at Saint Christophers, April, - -	1792
The Bread Fruit brought to St. Vincent by Capt. Bligh,	1793
Tobago taken by the English, April 15th, - -	..
Martinico taken by the English, March 22d, -	1794
Saint Lucia also taken April 4th, and Guadaloupe April 21st. retaken December 10th, - -	..
La Pique taken by the Blanche, Captain Falknor killed, January 5th, - - -	1795
Insurrection in Saint Vincent, March 5th, - -	..
The Maroons in Jamaica surrendered - -	1796
The Insurgents in Grenada surrendered, June 10th,	..
Spanish declaration of War against England, Oct. 5th,	..
Demerary, Esequibo, and Berbice surrendered to the English, April, - - -	..
Saint Lucia surrendered, May 26th -	..
The Caribs in Saint Vincent surrendered, and removed to Rattan, October, - - -	..

No. XXI. *continued.*

	A. D.
Trinidad surrendered to the British, February 17th,	1797
William Bentinck, Governor of St. Vincent, March 2d,	..
The British evacuated Saint Domingo, Toussaint declared Governor, October 26th, - - -	1798
Surinam capitulated, August 20th, - -	1799
Curaçoa capitulated, September 22d, - -	1800
The Lowestoffe and eight merchantmen lost of Inagua Grande - - - - -	..
Peace between England and France, October 1st,	1801
Dessalines's Treaty signed, March 27th, - -	1802
Tobago, Martinico, Saint Lucia, ceded to France, Demerary, Esequibo, Berbice, and Curaçoa to the Dutch, Trinidad to Great Britain - -	..
The 8th West India Regᵗ. mutinied at Dominica, April,	..
Henry William Bentinck, Governor of Saint Vincent, September 23d, - - - -	..
Saint Lucia and Tobago surrendered to the British, June, and Demerary, Esequibo, and Berbice in Sept.	1803
Dessalines General in Chief at Saint Domingo, Independence proclaimed, November 29th, - -	..
The Diamond Rock off Martinico fortified by Sir S. Wood, - - - - -	1804
Surinam taken, May 4th, - - -	..
Massacre of the White Inhabitants of Saint Domingo, April 29th, - - - - -	..
Hurricane at Saint Christophers, September, -	..
The French pillaged Dominica and Saint Christophers, February, - - -	1805
The Diamond Rock, commanded by Capt. Maurice, surrendered, June 14th, - - -	..
The Blanche taken by a French squadron, July 19th,	..
Sir George Beckwith, K. B. Governor of St. Vincent	1806
Admiral Duckworth's Victory off Saint Domingo, February 6th, - - - -	..
General Miranda's Expedition to the Main -	..
Act for the Abolition of the Slave Trade, May 23rd,	..
Great injury done to the Bahamas by gales of wind, September, - - - -	..
Hurricane at Dominica, September 9th, - -	..
Dessalines killed, and Pétion proclaimed President of Hayti, December 27th, - - -	..
Curaçoa taken by Captain, afterwards, Sir Charles Brisbane, January 1st, - - -	1807

No. XXI. *continued.*

	A. D.
Santa Crux and Saint Thomas surrendered to the British, December, - - -	1807
Marie Galante and Deseada surrendered - -	1808
Port of Spain, Trinidad, destroyed by Fire, April 24th,	..
Fire at Montego Bay, Jamaica, June, - -	..
Sir Charles Brisbane Governor of Saint Vincent, November 14th, - - - -	..
Henry Bentinck, Governor of Demerary and Esequibo, December 13th, - - - -	..
Peace between Great Britain and Spain, July 4th, -	..
Spanish part of Saint Domingo taken from the French by the English and Spanish forces -	1809
Cayenne surrendered to the British, January 12th,	..
Port of Spain again destroyed by Fire; £50,000. granted by Parliament to rebuild it - -	..
Martinico taken, February 24th, - -	..
The Saintes taken, April 17th, - -	..
Information of an intended Insurrection in Jamaica obtained from a deserter - - -	..
Junon frigate destroyed by two French frigates -	1809
Guadaloupe taken, January 27th, - -	1810
Saint Martins taken, February 14th, - -	..
Saint Eustatia and Saba, February 22nd, - -	..
Christophe, King of Hayti, by the name of Henry I.	1811
City of Carraccas destroyed by an Earthquake, March 26th, - - -	..
Arthur Hodge executed at Tortola for Murder -	..
Eruption of the Souffriere, St. Vincent, April 30th, -	1812
Earthquake at Jamaica, November; and a Hurricane, October, - - - -	1813
Castries, Saint Lucia, destroyed by fire, April 6th, -	..
Hurricanes in Dominica, July and August, -	..
General Peace: Tobago, Saint Lucia, Demerary, Esequibo, and Berbice retained by the British -	1814
Martinico and Guadaloupe occupied by the British for Louis XVIII. - - -	1815
Battle of Waterloo, and Flight of Buonaparte, June 18th, - - -	..
Fire at Port Royal, Jamaica, July 13th, - -	..
Treaty between the Allied Powers, November 20th,	..
Insurrection in Barbados, April 14th, - -	1816
Martinico and Guadaloupe restored to the French	..
The attack on Algiers, by Lord Exmouth, August,	..
Earthquake in Saint Vincent and Barbados, Dec. 23d,	..

No. XXI. *continued.*

	A. D.
Princess Charlotte of Wales died, November 6th, -	1817
Hurricane at St. Lucia and Martinique, October 21st,	..
Boyer succeeds Pétion at Saint Domingo, March, -	1818
Queen Charlotte died, November 17th, - -	..
Cession of the Floridas to the United States, -	1819
Fire at Saint John's, Newfoundland, July 19th, -	..
Hurricane in Antigua and the Leeward Islands -	..
Slave Registry Bill passed by the Imperial Parliament,	..
Republic of Columbia established, December, -	1820
Christophe (Henry I. of Hayti) destroyed himself -	..
Death of George III, and Accession of George IV· January 29th, - - - -	..
American Non-intercourse Act passed, May, -	..
The Church in Saint Vincent consecrated, Sept. 6th,	..
The Independence of South America acknowledged by the United States - - - -	1822
Wesleyan Chapel at Barbados destroyed by a mob	1823
Botanic Garden Establishment at Saint Vincent removed to Trinidad, May, - - -	..
Insurrection at Demerary among the Slaves -	..
Resolutions of the House of Commons respecting the amelioration of the Slave condition, May 16th,	..
Barbados and the Leeward Islands created into a Bishoprick, with two Archdeacons, March 16th,	1824
Conspiracy at Martinico discovered, - -	..
The Bishop arrived at Barbados - -	1825
Independence of Hayti recognised by France, -	..
Colonial Currency abolished in Tobago - -	..
The Laws of Trade and Navigation altered -	1825
Orders in Council respecting Slaves in Trinidad, -	..
Saint Thomas much injured by fire, February 12th,	..
Earthquake at Trinidad, September 20th, -	..
Branch Associations for the Instruction of Slaves established in the different Islands, -	1826
Earthquake at Santa Fé de Bogota, November 16th,	1827
Numerous piracies committed in the Leeward Islands,	1828
Twenty-eight Pirates executed at Saint Christophers, September, - - -	..

THE CASS LIBRARY OF WEST INDIAN STUDIES

As interest grew in the history and experiences of the black population of the world, attention increasingly focused on the islands of the Caribbean. Essential source material was largely inaccessible. In response to this interest Frank Cass Publishers have sought, through this series of reprints, to make available a thoroughly comprehensive selection of the historically most important 18th, 19th and early 20th century accounts and narratives. Supplementing these sources are works of more recent scholarship which have become out of print. These volumes are an invaluable source to scholars and students in this field as well as to those with a more general interest in the subject.

No. 1. George Wilson Bridges
The Annals of Jamaica (1828).
New Impression 1968 (ISBN 0-7146-1931-0)

No. 2. Anthony Trollope
The West Indies and the Spanish Main (1859; 1860).
New Impression 1968 (ISBN 0-7146-1953-1)

No. 3. William Sewell
The Ordeal of Free Labour in the West Indies (1861; 1862).
New Impression 1968 (ISBN 0-7146-1950-7)

No. 4. Thomas Southey
Chronological History of the West Indies (1827).
New Impression 1968 (ISBN 0-7146-1952-3)

No. 5. R. C. Dallas
The History of the Maroons, including the Expedition to Cuba and the Island of Jamaica (1803).
New Impression 1968 (ISBN 0-7146-1934-5)

No. 6. Frank Wesley Pitman
The Development of the British West Indies, 1700-1763 (1917).
New Impression 1967 (ISBN 0-7146-1109-3)

No. 7. Nellis Maynard Crouse
The French Struggle for the West Indies 1665-1713 (1943).
New Impression 1967 (ISBN 0-7146-1025-9)

No. 8. Jean Baptiste Labat
The Memoirs of Pere Labat 1693-1705
Translated by John Eaden (1931)
New Impression 1970 (ISBN 0-7146-1940-X)

No. 9. Henry H. Breen
St. Lucia: Historical, Statistical, and Descriptive (1844).
New Impression 1970 (ISBN 0-7146-1930-2)

No. 10. sir Robert Hermann Schomburgk
A Description of British Guiana. Geographical and Statistical; exhibiting its resources and capabilities, together with the present and future condition and prospects of the colony (1840).
New Impression 1970 (ISBN 0-7146-1949-3)

No. 11. Richard Ligon
A True and Exact History of the Island of Barbadoes. Illustrated with a Map of the Island, as also the Principal Trees and Plants there, set fourth in their due Proportions and Shapes, drawn out by their several respective scales. Together with the Ingenio that makes the Sugar etc., etc. (1657; 1673).
New Impression of the Second Edition 1970 (ISBN 0-7146-1941-8)

No. 12. Edward Long
The History of Jamaica, or General Survey of the Antient and Modern State of that Island; with Reflections on its Situation, Settlements, Inhabitants, Climate, Products, Commerce, Laws, and Government (1774).
With a new introduction by George Metcalf
New Edition 1970 (ISBN 0-7146-1942-6)

No. 13. E. L. Joseph
History of Trinidad (1838).
New Impression 1970 (ISBN 0-7146-1936-6)

No. 14. Alfred Caldecott
The Church in the West Indies (1898).
New Impression 1970 (ISBN 0-7146-1932-9)

No. 15. C. S. Salmon
The Caribbean Confederation. A plan for the union of the fifteen British West Indian Colonies, preceded by An Account of the Past and Present Condition of the European and the African Races Inhabiting them, with a true explanation of the Haytian Mystery (1888).
New Impression 1971 (ISBN 0-7146-1947-7)

No. 16. Lilliam M. Penson
The Colonial Agents of the British West Indies; a study in Colonial Administration, mainly in the Eighteenth Century (1924).
New Impression 1971 (ISBN 0-7146-1944-2)

No. 17. William James Gardner
A History of Jamaica from its Discovery by Christopher Columbus to the year 1872. Including an account of its trade and agriculture; sketches of the manners, habits and customs of all classes of its inhabitants; and a narrative of the progress of religion and education in the island (1909).
New Impression 1971 (ISBN 0-7146-1938-8)

No. 18. Sir William Young
An Account of the Black Charaibs in the Island of St. Vincent's (1795).
New Impression 1971 (ISBN 0-7146-1955-8)

No. 19. Sir Robert Hermann Schomburgk
The History of Barbados; composing a geographical and statistical description of the Island; a sketch of the historical events since the settlement; and an account of its geology and natural productions (1848).
New Impression 1971 (ISBN 0-7146-1948-5)

No. 20. Lionel Mordaunt Fraser
History of Trinidad from 1781 to 1839 (1891 and 1896).
New Impression 2 volumes 1971 (ISBN 0-7146-1937-X)

No. 21. Thomas Coke
A History of the West Indies, containing the Natural, Civil and Ecclesiastical History of each Island: with an account of the Missions which have been established in that Archipelago by the Society late in connexion with the Rev. John Wesley (1808-1811).
New Impression 3 volumes 1971 (ISBN 0-7146-1933-7)

No. 22. John Davy
The West Indies, before and since Slave Emancipation, comprising The Windward and Leeward Islands' Military Command; founded on notes and observations collected during a three years' residence (1854).
New Impression 1971 (ISBN 0-7146-1935-3)

No. 23. Charles Shephard
Historical Account of the Island of Saint Vincent (1831).
New Impression 1971 (ISBN 0-7146-1951-5)

No. 24. Richard Pares
War and Trade in the West Indies (1936).
New Impression 1963 (ISBN 0-7146-1943-4)

No. 25.
Not Published

No. 26. John Poyer
The History of Barbados, from the First Discovery of the Island, in the year 1605, till the Accession of Lord Seaforth, 1801 (1808).
New Impression 1971 (ISBN 0-7146-1945-0)

No. 27. Thomas Atwood
The History of the Island of Domonica. Containing a Description of its Situation, Extent, Climate, Mountains, Rivers, Natural Productions, etc. Together with An Account of the Civil Government, Trade, Laws, Customs, and Manners of the diffeerent inhabitants of that Island. Its Conquest by the French, and Restoration to the British Domonions (1791).
New Impression 1971 (ISBN 0-7146-1929-9)

No. 28. Henry Iles Woodcock
A History of Tobago (1867).
New Impression 1971 (ISBN 0-7146-2765-8)

For Product Safety Concerns and Information please contact our EU
representative GPSR@taylorandfrancis.com
Taylor & Francis Verlag GmbH, Kaufingerstraße 24, 80331 München, Germany